John S Hart

Thoughts on Sabbath-Schools

John S Hart

Thoughts on Sabbath-Schools

ISBN/EAN: 9783743324763

Manufactured in Europe, USA, Canada, Australia, Japa

Cover: Foto ©Lupo / pixelio.de

Manufactured and distributed by brebook publishing software (www.brebook.com)

John S Hart

Thoughts on Sabbath-Schools

THOUGHTS

ON

SABBATH-SCHOOLS

BY

JOHN S. HART, LL.D.

PHILADELPHIA:
PRESBYTERIAN BOARD OF PUBLICATION,
No. 821 Chestnut Street.

Entered according to the Act of Congress, in the year 1864, by

THE TRUSTEES OF THE

PRESBYTERIAN BOARD OF PUBLICATION,

In the Clerk's Office of the District Court for the Eastern District of Pennsylvania.

STEREOTYPED BY WILLIAM W. HARDING.

CONTENTS.

CHAPTER	PAGE
I. The Sabbath-School as a Philanthropic Enterprise,	7
II. Church Members and the Sabbath-School,	10
III. Relation of the Sabbath-School to the Family,	15
IV. The Relation of the Pastor to the Sabbath-School,	23
V. The Sabbath-School and the Pulpit,	27
VI. The Tendency of the Sabbath-School to Promote Christian Union,	32
VII. The Sabbath-School Work exhaustive of its Subject,	36
VIII. A Lion in the Path,	40
IX. Working alone and Working together,	45
X. The Long Vacation,	50
XI. Attendance of Sabbath-School Children upon Church,	54
XII. How to keep the Older Scholars,	62
XIII. Graded Sabbath-Schools,	67
XIV. Church Architecture and Sabbath-Schools,	78
XV. Infant-Schools,	83
XVI. The Use of Books in Infant-Schools,	88

CONTENTS.

CHAPTER		PAGE
XVII.	Music in Sabbath-Schools,	92
XVIII.	Sabbath-School Books and Papers,	98
XIX.	The Sabbath-School Library,	104
XX.	Sabbath-Schools and Christian Missions,	113
XXI.	The Sabbath-School Superintendent,	124
XXII.	The Teacher—Love for the Work,	130
XXIII.	The Teacher's Preparation for his Class,	134
XXIV.	Punctuality in Teachers,	140
XXV.	Irregular Attendance of Teachers,	146
XXVI.	Duty of the Teacher in regard to Class Order,	153
XXVII.	Filling up the Time,	159
XXVIII.	Visiting Scholars,	165
XXIX.	The Teacher's Daily Walk,	172
XXX.	The Teacher's Aim,	177
XXXI.	The Influence of the Sabbath-School Work on the Teacher,	185
XXXII.	The Employment of Persons as Teachers in Sabbath-Schools who are not Professors of Religion,	190
XXXIII.	The Use of Question Books and Commentaries to Teachers,	196
XXXIV.	Teaching Children what they do not Understand,	201
XXXV.	Faith as an Educational Power,	206
XXXVI.	The Proper Use of Authority in Teaching,	211

PREFACE.

There is no more effectual way of finding out what are the real questions which the Sabbath-school worker has to meet, than to follow up a series of Sabbath-school Conventions. There are certain topics which invariably come up at these meetings. Whether the Convention be a union of different denominations, or a meeting of the Sabbath-school men of one particular denomination, whether it be a County, a State, or a National Convention, these topics are sure to appear. The reason is obvious. The practical wants and difficulties and encouragements of Sabbath-school teachers are pretty much the same all the world over. When they come together in council, they come not to discuss abstract theories, but as earnest men, with a practical end in view. Hence their conferences almost invariably involve pretty much the same circle of ideas. By a little change of dates and names, the report of one Convention would answer for the report of almost any other Convention.

It has been my duty and privilege to study carefully almost every Sabbath-school Convention, of any considerable size or importance, which has been held in the last five or six years. Believing that I have thus become pretty well acquainted with the topics which at this time have a real and living interest for the Sabbath-school worker, I have hoped to contribute my mite towards the great cause by giving to these topics a brief consideration. My aim has been, not to waste time and space with irrelevant matter, or in mere circumlocution, or to write a methodical and systematic treatise, which would require a large volume, but to touch only on those points which are of practical interest, and in each case to touch directly upon what seemed to be the vital point in the matter. The book, therefore, is strictly and properly a collection of "Thoughts," as expressed in the title. Yet the reader will find, on examination, that these "Thoughts" have a real though not a formal connection, and that they go over pretty much the whole subject, involving questions concerning the moral, religious, and ecclesiastical relations of Sabbath-schools, their establishment, organization, and management, and the qualifications and duties of teachers.

I do not profess to bring forward anything specially new. My humble aim is rather to be a faithful exponent and reporter of the admitted creed of those who have had most experience in this great field of evangelic effort.

THOUGHTS ON SABBATH-SCHOOLS.

I.

THE SABBATH-SCHOOL AS A PHILANTHROPIC ENTERPRISE.

The main ground of support for the Sabbath-school is drawn from its religious character. At the same time, it has claims upon the good-will, the confidence, and the co-operation of men who are not religious. No man who wishes to be thought a good citizen, who would be thought a philanthropist or a patriot, should withhold his countenance and support from this enterprise. No conviction is more assured, in the minds of those who have had opportunities of observation, than that the Sabbath-school is one of the most powerful and efficient means of promoting morality. Whatever promotes good morals, by the same ratio lessens crime, and by consequence lessens taxation, pauperism, vagrancy, and all the long train of social and political evils which are the prolific progeny of crime.

These truths are now considered self-evident. But there has been a further discovery. There is no agency like the Sabbath-school for restoring to decency and purity those depraved neighbourhoods that have sunk apparently below the reach of redemption.

In every city and town, and almost in every country neighbourhood, there is usually some one plague spot, some corner or rookery, where wickedness is rife. So well has the influence of the Sabbath-school come to be understood, as a healer of social pollution, that now, in many places, the political authorities, not indeed in their official capacities as mayors or magistrates, but as patriotic and philanthropic men, are striving to abate these social nuisances by planting Sabbath-schools right in the midst of them. Even the Five Points of New York, which had for more than half a century bid defiance to the law, has yielded at length to the ameliorating influence of the gospel.

If it is patriotic and wise to expend money and energy in the support of secular schools, and of Houses of Refuge and Reform, the argument is much stronger in favour of the Sabbath-school.

There are persons in every community, who excuse themselves from active co-operation in the Sabbath-school work, on the ground that they are not members of the church and do not feel qualified to give religious instruction. Others excuse themselves on the plea of feeble health, or unavoidable domestic engagements. Our present business is not with the validity of these excuses. There is one thing which these people usually may do. They may at least contribute to the support of the institution. The Sabbath-school necessarily costs something,—not much, indeed, but something; and it is surely not meet that those who do all the work should also meet all the expenses, as is too often the case. Library books are needed, question-books, hymn-books, children's papers, teachers' papers, fixtures of various kinds, all of which require money. The main item of expense indeed is wanting, the tuition being free. But the other items, though small, infinitesimally small compared with the benefits accruing, yet do exist and must be met. No Sabbath-school can be conducted with a full degree of efficiency and power, without an annual expenditure of about one dollar for every scholar.

Here then is an opportunity for the exercise of philanthropy and public spirit on the part of those gentlemen and ladies who for reasons satisfactory to themselves withhold their own personal services from the work. Mission-schools particularly need pecuniary assistance. If you will not bestow your labour, bestow of your substance to this work. If you cannot teach, give. Help those self-denying men and women who are teaching.

II.

CHURCH MEMBERS AND THE SABBATH-SCHOOL.

Has a church member, as such, any necessary relation to the Sabbath-school? Is this cause one which a professing Christian may, or may not, at his option, support? Is it, in short, in the present state of the church and the world, something which affects the question of personal duty of every professed follower of Jesus? No one can fail to see that this question goes to the very quick. On the answer which the church shall give, depends mainly the success of the Sabbath-school cause.

The true child of God cannot feel entire indifference to any effort of benevolence affecting the welfare of man. There are some enterprises, however, which touch him only remotely and indirectly, and in common with others who are not Christians. It would be difficult, for instance, to establish a claim of universal obligation upon every Christian, as such, to join in the establishment and supervision of a Soup Society, or a Prison Discipline Society, or of very many other things which affect mainly mere temporal wants, and the interests of society. It might be difficult to establish such a claim even for the Sabbath-school, taking it to be merely such an institution as was in the mind of its benevolent founder, Robert Raikes. But in the Providence of God, the Sabbath-school has become one of the leading agencies of the church in carrying forward the work of evangelizing the world. It is no longer a mere plan for keeping poor neglected children out of the street, and teaching them to read and spell on the Sabbath-day. It aims indeed to do this, but it aims also to do a hundred fold more. Temporal benefits undoubtedly flow from the Sabbath-school, especially to the poorer classes. Wherever it flourishes, there order prevails, manners are improved, decorum, industry, economy, thrift, a desire to become respectable, a love of reading, and a general thirst for knowledge, gain ground. But these are the incidental results of the Sabbath-school teacher's work. They are not his chief aim. What he mainly and primarily seeks is the conversion of his scholars. He seeks to make them true Christians, knowing that if this point be gained, all other needed things "will be added." Conversion is the need of every soul, of the rich as well as of the poor. Here is a want which includes all. Hence the Sabbath-school seeks to gather into its fold the children of all classes. No children are too high, none are too low, to be beyond its benefits. As a matter of fact, a large part of those now converted to God and brought into the church on profession of their faith, come from the Sabbath-school. At a

State Sabbath-school Convention, in Lawrence, Mass., the question being moved, with a view to bring out this significant fact, all those persons were requested to rise who had been converted while attending Sabbath-school. Almost the entire assembly rose. At least nine-tenths of the Convention were on their feet.

It is not claimed, from such facts as these, that the Sabbath-school by itself, as an independent agency, apart from the church and the ministry, is an institution to be relied upon for the conversion of the world. What indeed makes the Sabbath-school, what gives it life and being, but the church and the ministry? What is the Sabbath-school, but the church and the ministry working in that particular way? Christ's ministers and his people find that a given amount of labour yields larger returns, when put forth among the young than when put forth among the old. The young are more tender-hearted; they are more easily influenced; they have fewer evil habits to be broken up; their habits are not so stubborn; the world has not yet such a controlling influence over them; appeals to conscience, exhibitions of the love of Christ, arguments from the glories or the terrors of the world to come, have more hold upon them. Hence labour for their conversion is more hopeful. The minister does not indeed despair of the aged. He labours and he prays for the old as well as for the young. But he finds his chief encouragement among the latter.

Here too, more than elsewhere, he can have the co-operation of his people. Almost every godly man and woman in his flock can help him in his labour among the little ones. But among the adults, among the parents of those very children, he must work almost alone. Scores may be found in every church, able and willing to preach Christ to the child of the hardened worldling. But who shall be found with the courage and the discretion to go with the same message to the father himself, to the ungodly lawyer, physician, or merchant?

If such, then, be the aim and object of the Sabbath-school, if it be in fact, not some outside, philanthropic association, but the church itself working in a particular way, for the better husbanding of its resources, there can be no doubt of the duty of every professing Christian to give it his support. As a member of Christ's church, he is consecrated to its service, and here is a particular service in which the church finds her labours towards the conversion of the world most efficient. There are undoubtedly some professing Christians who are not required to engage personally as Sabbath-school teachers. Bodily infirmity, more imperative duties in the family or elsewhere, and other causes, may forbid such a service. But the cause of the Sabbath-school has assumed such magnitude and proportions, in the grand aggressive movements of the church, that the fact of entering the church should be considered *prima facie* evidence of an intention to enter the Sabbath-school, if one is not already there. Every one proposing to join the church, should distinctly propose to himself the question, What shall I do for the Sabbath-school? Ministers and sessions, in admitting persons to the church, should ask the candidate, What are you going to do for the Lord in this part of his vineyard? The question of personal duty in the matter should be presented and pressed to a conscientious and deliberate decision. It should not be, it is not, a matter about which a professing Christian may be indifferent.

III.

RELATION OF THE SABBATH-SCHOOL TO THE FAMILY.

Has the Sabbath-school a tendency to supersede parental training? So it has been alleged by some, and the allegation, if true, is one of grave import.

No charge against the Sabbath-school system has given more real solicitude. It has disturbed the minds not of the thoughtless, the indifferent, or the worldly, but of the truly devout. The time is remembered, when the father gathered his household around him on the evening of the Sabbath, and gave them instruction on religious subjects. This custom, if maintained at all, is not so common as it once was, and it is feared by many that the cause of its going out of fashion has been the Sabbath-school. Parents, finding an institution in existence which professed to care for the religious instruction of the children, have been only too willing to accept the school as a substitute for their own instructions.

If such a tendency exists, or wherever it exists, it should be by all means resisted. The Sabbath-school was never designed to supersede family instruction. It is an aid, an addition, a supplement to what the father and mother can do. But no device of man can do away with the parental obligation. No duty of the parent is more solemn or inalienable than that of seeing personally to the religious instruction of his offspring. He may with as good a right delegate to the soup society the duty of supplying his children with food, as he may throw off upon any shoulders the duty of seeing that his children grow up in the fear of God, and in the knowledge of the Christian religion. Sabbath-school teachers and superintendents, therefore, in conducting their operations, should be careful to resist any tendency of this kind, when they see it. There are undoubtedly multitudes of parents, who have no sense of obligation on the subject, or what little they may have, is easily satisfied by allowing their children to go to the school. But these same parents would do no better, if there were no Sabbath-school. They have no sense of religion themselves, and they have no serious care that their children should have. The custom of family catechetical instruction on the Sabbath has undoubtedly gone very much out of use. But so have many other excellent customs. The question is, not whether parents are careless, or neglectful, but whether the Sabbath-school tends to make them so. If the testimony of pastors and teachers on this point could be collected, I believe it would be clear and decided,

First, That it is not the design of the Sabbath-school to supersede parental training and instruction, to weaken the bonds of parental authority, or to deaden the sense of parental obligation; but, on the contrary, to stimulate parents to increased fidelity, and children to a higher standard of filial duty; *Secondly*, as a fact, that, in those congregations and communities in which the Sabbath-school is in most vigorous and healthful operation, family religion is likewise in most healthy and vigorous condition.

No men as a class are greater sticklers for parental responsibilities than Sabbath-school men. We hold it as a first, most elementary, most indisputable truth, that the parent has a responsibility for the moral and religious training of his child, from which no auxiliary and supplementary agency can release him. It is our aim as Sabbath-school teachers to quicken in the parent's mind the sense of this obligation. The greatest difficulty in our work is the feeling of unconcern which so many parents have on this subject. We feel that we have reached our highest result, when we have gained not only the children, but through them the parents also. If any of our measures are found in any instances to make the parent feel that the Sabbath-school is to take the children off his hands, and leave him nothing to do, and nothing to answer for before God, no men are so willing as we to correct the mistake. None have such an interest as we in the correction. If every head of a family were a

Christian, who recognised the obligation to train up his children in the fear of the Lord, and who had the education and the intellectual qualifications necessary for giving them instruction in religious truth, the duty of Christian men and women in this matter would be very different from what it now is.

But we cannot shut our eyes to the fact that the vast majority of parents are persons who care nothing for religion themselves, and that many of them, even if religious themselves, would be very poorly qualified to give instruction to their children. We cannot shut our ears to the solemn injunction of our Lord, "Feed my lambs." We believe it to be a most solemn duty of the church to look after the young, not those merely within her own household, but all the little neglected ones within her reach. A child is growing up in sin. Unless properly cared for, it will fall a prey to Satan, and go down to everlasting death. Who is guilty before God of this result? The parent undoubtedly. But so also is the church, that stands by and sees the little one perish without putting out a helping hand to save it.

The fact that the parent is guilty, does not make the church any the less guilty. Christ holds both responsible. But, says a Christian professor, I believe fully what you say. Let the Sabbath-school look after the neglected children. The work is a good one. I bid it God-speed. It has my best wishes and my prayers. Do all you can for those children whose parents will not themselves undertake their training. For myself, however, I teach my own children at home, in the old-fashioned way. My children do not attend the schools as scholars, nor I as a teacher, for my home-teaching takes all the time I can give to the subject. But you, who are engaged in the school, will have one family the less to look after.

Let us canvass this a little.

If one Christian may with a good conscience take this ground, so may every other, and our whole system of Sabbath-school instruction falls to the ground. There is no obligation on me to leave my own family and teach in the Sabbath-school, that is not on him. There is no propriety or occasion for my children's attending as scholars, that does not apply with equal force to his. Withdraw from the Sabbath-school the children of Christian households, and the services of Christian men and women of experience and education, and where are we? The very man, who thus excuses himself from serving in the Sabbath-school, and his children from going, because he is competent to train them himself, and feels the obligation to do so, is the one most needed in the school, and his family is the one whose influence in the school is most needed to countenance and encourage others. Are we to leave the school to be managed mainly by the young, the inexperienced, the irreligious, the morally and intellectually incompetent? Such must be the result, if every parent like the one named, may be excused from the work. What will be the character of the school itself, if no children attend but the neglected ones of the community? Will the parents of even such children be willing to let them attend, if it comes to be understood that going to Sabbath-school is a badge of parental ignorance and neglect?

There is a selfishness in the position taken by the Christian professor just quoted, which it is difficult to reconcile with the teachings of that charity which "seeketh not her own." Paul says, "Let no man seek his own, but every man another's" welfare. "Look not every man on his own things, but also on the things of others." "Not seeking mine own profit, but the profit of many, that they may be saved." "Be ye followers of me, even as I am also of Christ." Did Christ shut himself up in his own home, and confine his teaching and his deeds of mercy to his own kindred?

The duty of teaching in the Sabbath-school is not, like that of the ministry, a special mission to be undertaken by a chosen few. If society is to be thoroughly evangelized, it requires the active, self-denying efforts of the whole body of Christians. There are exceptional cases, as of confirmed invalids, mothers with young children, and so forth. But with these exceptions, which no one gainsays, it is the duty of all, and of one no less than another, to engage in direct personal efforts to bring the unevangelized portion of the community under the influence of gospel truth. The Sabbath-school, as an evangelizing agency, has this peculiarity, that it is a place for every one. In that blessed institution, every man, woman, and child may be useful, who has a mind to the work.

"But," says the professor before quoted, "have I not a primary duty to my own family? Shall not I, who can do it, teach my own children? Why should I lay the burden of teaching my children upon those of you who are engaged in teaching the children of parents who cannot, or who will not, teach them?"

Is the discharge of a primary duty any excuse for the neglect of a secondary one? Do you suppose, moreover, that we, who take our families with us to the Sabbath-school, do not also teach them at home just as much, and as regularly as you do? Our children have lessons to recite in their several classes. We feel it to be our duty to see to it during the week, and on the Sabbath, that they learn these lessons. We go over the lessons with them, and assist them in the preparation.

After thus doing all we can by home influence and instruction for the benefit of our children, we are grateful that they may have the additional benefit of the instruction, the prayers, and the Christian counsels of their Sabbath-school teacher. The very familiarity of home is often a barrier to the personal application of the truth to the conscience of the child. A teacher has at times a freedom in addressing a child on the subject of personal religion, which the parent finds it difficult to command. Children, moreover, are social and sympathetic in their natures. Lessons which would be dry and irksome, when plodded over alone, become agreeable and interesting when pursued amid the excitement of pleasant companionship. We wish our children in their religious learning to have the advantage of this companionship, which we have found so beneficial in other studies. If you would follow Paul even as he followed Christ (neither of them very pertinent examples of your spirit of isolation); if you would really have the blessing of Christ on your family and on your own soul,—do not indeed cease to teach and train your children at home, (far be it from any Sabbath-school man to give you such advice),—but, having done your own duty thoroughly to them at home, then bring them with you to the Sabbath-school, and there hope for them, while you give to others, that additional blessing which comes from voluntary, self-denying, associated action in the cause of Christ.

IV.

THE RELATION OF THE PASTOR TO THE SABBATH-SCHOOL.

There is truth, if not the whole truth, in Dr. Tyng's position on this subject. The pastor of a church is the natural, perpetual, *ex-officio* superintendent of its Sabbath-school. Few pastors, indeed, have the physical strength, even where they have every other qualification, to go through the details of actual supervision, as Dr. Tyng does. Yet every pastor, who is wise, will keep himself in constant, living contact with his school. He should be in it some portion of the time every Sabbath. He need not burden himself with the care of minute supervision. But he should know every teacher, and if possible, every scholar. He should know what is going on in the school, what they are studying, what hymns they sing, what they are doing in the way of benevolence. He should every Sabbath catch fire from the warm, young hearts there assembled, and let his own heart give back an answering glow. He should move in and out among the classes in kindly and genial sympathy, giving and catching sunshine by his presence. A half hour so spent by the pastor is better preparation for the pulpit than studying points of elocution in his chamber, or practising posture and gesticulation before his mirror.

That in which preaching usually is most deficient, is want of sympathy between the speaker and his hearers. There is often an awful, impassable gulf between the pulpit and the pew. The familiar intercourse of the school-room helps to bridge over this gulf. The teachers and the children, who form no inconsiderable part of the congregation, feel that the speaker in that distant pulpit is not so far off, after all. He is the same kind friend who has just given them a cordial greeting, a pleasant smile, a warm pressure of the hand. His words come to them as a fresh coinage from the heart.

This is not all. The effect is still more marked upon the speaker. The preacher cannot help being warmed up with his solemn message, when delivering it to those among whom he has just been mingling in loving and familiar intercourse. Not only by this constant intercourse with his school, is the minister's heart warmed and set aglow for the actual delivery of his sermon, but the school furnishes him with a perennial source of subjects for discourse. There are two volumes in which the minister finds his text. One is in the leaves of his Bible, the other is in the hearts of his people. No portion of his people open their hearts with so warm and ready a sympathy as those in the Sabbath-school. There the practiced eye of the wise and thoughtful pastor sees what truths most need present illustration and support, what errors need to be refuted, what influences are to be resisted, what mining is to be countermined, when the promises, when the warnings of the gospel are to be pressed. The school is to him the unerring pulse by which the life of the great congregation may be read, and its spiritual wants predicated.

I have never known a Sabbath-school, in which the pastor thus regularly identified himself with its general life and movement, which did not yield abundant fruits in the way of conversions and additions to the church. It is hardly possible, in the nature of things, that preaching under such circumstances can be without fruit. The school furnishes the sunshine and the rain, under whose genial influences the soil is best prepared and the seed most surely germinates.

In every community, there are families, worldly people, who are not connected with any church, who attend statedly no place of worship. The pastor finds in his Sabbath-school just the agency for bringing such families within the pale of gospel influences, and finally within the church. Children are naturally social and gregarious. The children of worldly parents are easily drawn into the school. If the pastor is there to meet the children and to win their love, the way is not far to the hearts of the parents. I believe the records of every growing church will show that more families from the world are brought into the church by the agency of the Sabbath-school, than by all other causes. But in order to the school producing such results, it must enjoy the continual presence and the active co-operation of the pastor.

V.

THE SABBATH-SCHOOL AND THE PULPIT.

THERE is no more mischievous error, in regard to the Sabbath-school, than to suppose that there is, or can be, any divorce between it and the pulpit. The pulpit is the appointed and recognised centre of religious influence and interest in each congregation. Wherever there is not the most entire harmony and sympathy between the Sabbath-school and the minister, wherever the Sabbath-school does not find in the pastor its warmest friend and its most steadfast and efficient support, wherever the minister does not find in his Sabbath-school teachers his most reliable fellow-workers, or does not find his Sabbath-school the most inviting spot in all his spiritual garden,—there is something wrong.

When any one of these evil conditions exists, it is not always easy to say how it shall be remedied. One thing is certain. It is not to be done by scolding and fault-finding. Indeed, that is about the very poorest remedy ever tried for any thing. If you think your minister does not care enough about your school, if you seldom see him there, or if, when he is there, he shows no interest, or has no kind word of sympathy or greeting for you or your scholars, be assured, you will not mend the matter by going about in the congregation uttering complaints and creating discontent. There are ministers, possibly, who regard their Sabbath-schools with indifference, as something outside from the regular work of Christianizing the masses. But the number of such is now very small, and is yearly becoming smaller. I fear the number is greater of teachers and superintendents, who think the school is an outside organization, quite independent of the church and the minister. Such a feeling is assuredly wrong. The Sabbath-school is one of the modes by which the people of God, in their associated capacity as a church or a congregation, work together in spreading the gospel. Of all such action, the minister and the usual church authorities are the natural and rightful head and source of control. The more a congregation, in any of its benevolent operations, is interpenetrated with this spirit of unity, the more healthy and vigorous will it be.

The ways by which a minister may make himself felt in the Sabbath-school, are many and various. Some may directly superintend the school. This, however, is rarely the case. Nor is it ordinarily desirable. It has worked admirably, no doubt, in some cases. But they are rare. Most ministers have not the gifts, in addition to their other and more important duties, to exercise the direct supervision of a Sabbath-school. Besides, were they to do so, it might be at the expense of failing to call into exercise the unoccupied talents of some layman. One of the beauties of the Sabbath-school system is that it gives occupation to the entire talent of the church, lay as well as clerical.

A clergyman misses a great privilege, and fails to reach a large element of religious power in his congregation, who does not spend some portion of every Sabbath in his Sabbath-school. I do not mean that he should harangue his school every Sabbath. Having a long and heavy work for his voice immediately before him in the pulpit, he might not always find it safe to be addressing the school beforehand. But a *visit* to his school, so far from fatiguing, would be sure to refresh and animate him. It would warm his heart, give new tone and vigour to his emotions, and make his pulpit service more full of life and power. It is the habit of some ministers, when the school is held before church, always to enter it soon after the school is opened, and pass quietly round from class to class, giving a grasp of the hand to one, a smile to another, a kind word to another, becoming acquainted with the scholars, learning the wants of individuals, receiving from teachers information as to the spiritual condition of one and another of their scholars, mingling their sympathies with the afflicted and the tempted, and teaching all from the oldest to the youngest, to look up to their minister as their certain, unfailing friend. The minister, not having the care of governing and superintending the school on his hands, can thus spend an hour most profitably to himself and to his flock, with no appreciable addition to his labours.

One reason why so few pastors thus statedly visit their schools, is the idea they have that they will always be expected to make an address. Many superintendents frighten their pastors out of the school by insisting on making them speak when they get them there. Another reason, I fear, is the habit some ministers have of postponing their pulpit preparations till the last moment. The preacher often needs Sunday morning to revise and study his sermon, and therefore cannot visit his school, if he would.

There is no plainer ministerial duty than that of preaching occasionally on the subject of Sabbath-schools, and also of preaching to the Sabbath-school. That any minister should forego such an occasion and such a topic, argues a degree of short-sightedness that is perfectly amazing. There is hardly any branch of the Sabbath-school work on which the congregation do not need, and on which they have not a right to expect, admonition and instruction from the pulpit. They need to be stirred up to the duty of giving the school a liberal support. The duties of parents and teachers need to be expounded. The necessity of missionary efforts outside of the congregation, needs to be set forth and urged upon the people. The other duty, that of preaching sermons occasionally to the children, is equally plain. No ministerial labour ordinarily brings so large and so prompt a return.

VI.

THE TENDENCY OF THE SABBATH-SCHOOL TO PROMOTE CHRISTIAN UNION.

I am not of the number of those who suppose that all churches are to be merged in one. I see no reason why Christians may not be grouped in different families, with names and peculiarities suited to each. God has not made men all alike. He does not make Christians alike. They differ physically, mentally, morally, spiritually. As upon the earth there are differences of climate and soil, upland and lowland, mountain and valley, arctic regions and torrid, and races of men suited by physical organization to inhabit each, so it would seem as if, in the church, the great Proprietor did not intend a monotonous uniformity, but rather has sent diversities of operations in this, as in all his other works. The fact that the church is divided off into different sects, with varying names and banners, need not in the least impair its efficiency, any more than the separation into different camps, brigades and regiments, should impair the efficiency of an army. Let those Christians worship and work together, whose spiritual affinities so incline them. What is wanted, in order to true Christian union, is, not that all Christians should think and feel and act exactly alike in every minute particular,—they cannot do so, if they would, any more than they can all *look* alike—but that they should all strive for the same great end, the glory of Christ, that they should love all who bear his name and image, and that they should cultivate the disposition to regard more the great points in which all Christians agree, than those minor points in which they differ.

One of the blessed tendencies of the Sabbath-school is that it promotes this kind of union. It does so in various ways. In the first place, in every Sabbath-school, even those most strictly denominational and most under direct ecclesiastical control, there are always children belonging to families having different ecclesiastical connections or proclivities. The teachers are brought into communication with these families, and the intercourse, both in and out of school, serves to beget liberal and charitable feelings on both sides, and to dissipate the prejudices arising from a habit of seclusion. This is particularly true in mission schools in cities, and in union schools in the pioneer regions of the interior, where teachers of different religious names join in the establishment and support of a school. Christians thus uniting in the work of doing good, are warmed with love to each other, and are surprised to find how greatly the points which they hold in common exceed those in which they differ.

However it may be accounted for, there is something in the Sabbath-school work, which begets Christian fellowship and brotherly love. In the same church, none usually are knit together so closely, or have such cordial relations, as the fellow-teachers in the Sabbath-school. There is something in the work of caring for the spiritual interests of children that awakens the best feelings of our nature. Children, too, are wonderfully alike, the world over. In reading of the Sabbath-schools at Aintab, at Constantinople, at Alexandria, at Jerusalem, at Lodiana, the teacher finds his own joys and trials brought fresh to mind, as if reading of schools in New York or Philadelphia. So, too, when teachers of different churches or denominations come together in conventions or anniversaries, the experience of each finds a response in the hearts of all. They are like pilgrims who meet at an inn, after having passed at different hours over the same road. They feel like brothers, because they find by comparison that they have so much experience in common. Nothing is more remarkable, in looking over the report of a Sabbath-school convention, than to see how uniformly the topics for discussion, and the general proceedings, are alike. Indeed, by some little skill in changing names and dates, a report of one convention might very well pass for the report of half a dozen others. This fact, which often takes from the interest of the report, adds to the interest of the meeting itself. For nothing gives greater pleasure to social gatherings of any kind than a sense of community of feelings and interests among the members.

The truth is, children are the same the world over, in heathen as well as in Christian lands, and the work of labouring for their conversion is essentially the same, and is besides a work which so calls forth the best affections of the Christian heart, that fellow-labourers in the blessed cause when brought together in Sabbath-school festivals, celebrations, anniversaries, and conventions, as they frequently are, are led to love each other as brethren, and to feel with special force how blessed a thing it is for brethren to dwell together in unity.

VII.

THE SABBATH-SCHOOL WORK EXHAUSTIVE OF ITS SUBJECT.

The Sabbath-school work has one feature that ought to be kept continually in mind. It is capable, when fully carried out, of *exhausting* the subject, that is, of leaving no item in the great mass untouched and unaffected. It is eminently pervading and permeating, reaching to the smallest, the most remote, and the most minute. The work of the pulpit is different in this respect. The preacher makes indeed public proclamation to all. But, in the first place, this proclamation is addressed mainly to adults, and is little understood except by adults. In the second place, it is heard only by those who attend church. The neglecters of religion, those who most need the gospel, are not present to hear its offers. It is notorious that the preacher's voice does not and can not reach one half of the community. Even in those denominations, which by means of an itinerancy come nearest towards reaching the entire mass of the people, there is still always an outstanding element unreached.

The Sabbath-school is no substitute for the pulpit. But it is the pulpit's most important auxiliary, and it can do service beyond the reach of the pulpit's influence. It can carry out to the minutest extremities of the system the pulsations received from that mighty central power. The pulpit is the heart, the Sabbath-school is the arteries and veins. It is an apparatus by which the streams of influence may be divided and subdivided, until in its minute ramifications the net-work covers the entire surface, so that not a point shall be left unpervaded.

Stick a pin into any part of the human body and you draw blood, showing that a vein is there. The human circulation is exhaustive of its subject; it leaves not a point unreached. So the Sabbath-school is a machinery capable of exhausting its subject,—of reaching every child in the community. It is capable of an efficiency, a thoroughness, afforded by no other benevolent agency. The Sabbath-school teacher, having but a small number of little ones to look after, can look individually after every one of his class, adapting his means to the wants of each, and following each to his home. The business of gathering in the children that are out of the Sabbath-school is also a work of individual, personal labour. It is not to be done in the mass, like preaching a sermon to a thousand people. It is a strictly missionary work, to be done from house to house, and from child to child. There are neighbourhoods where this exhaustive process is carried into practical efficiency by those who direct the Sabbath-school machinery. The district is mapped off geographically, into minute sections, until each teacher-visitor has only five or six families to look after, and then every child of suitable age is pressed into the school, if willing to go. In such a district not a child is left uncared for.

There are neighbourhoods where this result is substantially reached. It may be so reached in every neighbourhood where the Christian people will apply the machinery put at their disposal. The Sabbath-school does certainly furnish an agency by which, in the easiest, most pleasant, most economical, and most efficient way, a sound gospel influence may be carried to every household of the community.

There is, in this matter, a special duty incumbent on those Christians who settle in pioneer regions, or districts destitute of preaching and of religious ordinances. Nothing is easier than to start a Sabbath-school. It need not be a large school. If it includes only your own child and one or two of your neighbour's children, it is still a school, and it will grow. It is a nucleus around which good influences will gather. Make a beginning, no matter how small or humble, and look to God for results.

As "two or three" are a Scriptural quorum for a prayer-meeting, so any number beyond one is sufficient to constitute a Sabbath-school; and wherever there is even one neglected child, it is the duty of Christ's people to look after it and bring it under the influence of religious instruction.

VIII.

A LION IN THE PATH.

No important end, good or bad, is ever reached without meeting obstacles. The tendency of the timid and the weak-hearted is to overrate those obstacles, to magnify them into devouring lions. But like the lions before Bunyan's Pilgrim, a bold and resolute advance, in a majority of cases, shows that they are chained, or else are old and toothless, or that they are merely some innocent and harmless creatures dressed up in the lion's skin.

Whoever enters upon the Sabbath-school work, in any of its departments, must expect to encounter difficulties. Especially when the friends of the enterprise undertake to give to the work the exhaustive character which I have spoken of, will they find all sorts of pretended impossibilities arrayed before them.

The Sabbath-school visitor will have to enter houses of the most forbidding character. In the house of the inebriate, the unclean, the thief, the criminal of every dye, are children who, by labour and love, may be rescued from the degradation and the wretchedness of their miserable parents. The refined and gentle may shrink from contact with such scenes. Besides the repulsiveness of the work, its actual danger is alarming. To reach some children, it is necessary to go into the midst of scenes of violence, where neither person nor property is quite safe. It requires stout nerves, no less than a strong love, to work for Christ in such places. The lion in the path is appalling. Yet we see persons of the greatest refinement and gentleness of character, ladies no less than gentlemen, perhaps more frequently than gentlemen, going boldly forward into the very lowest haunts of vice and crime, in search of the neglected little ones. If such workers for Christ are questioned in regard to their work, the uniform answer is, that the difficulty and danger diminish on a nearer approach. There is something in the nature of the errand of the Sabbath-school visitor that appeals to whatever is left of generous or good in the depraved heart, and there are few hearts in which the embers of goodness are quite extinct. There is one spark at least, even beneath the ashes in which all the other lovely traits of character have been consumed. Kindness shown to their children sometimes softens hearts that seemed utterly hardened. The Sabbath-school teacher in such haunts often receives a genuine welcome, when any other benefactor would be repelled with coarse ribaldry, if not with personal violence. There are instances, indeed, especially where the degradation comes from intempe-

4 *

rance, in which even parental love is obliterated. But such instances are rare. Even the most vicious and degraded usually wish better things for their children, and are grateful to those whose mission of mercy is to the little ones.

The lion is sometimes found in quite the opposite direction. A person who goes without fear or scruple into the very lowest walks of life, on his errand of mercy, pauses long before the threshold of the rich and cultivated infidel or worldling. In that lower walk of beneficence, are no embarrassing questions of ceremony and etiquette. Suppose the teachers of a certain district have determined to bring into the Sabbath-school every child within the district, who is willing, and whose parents are willing, that he should attend. They resolve, for this purpose, to make a thorough exploration. They go through the lanes and alleys. They explore the tenement houses and the cellars. Shall the stately mansion be passed by? Is not the child of wealth, if growing up in ignorance of the way of salvation, to be pitied, as well as the child of poverty? Families thoroughly godless are to be found in the upper walks of life, as well as in the lower, and no work of evangelization is thorough and exhaustive which does not include the means of reaching these ungodly rich people. The task is not easy, and it is not to be undertaken by every one. Yet such people are not insensible to unpretending, sincere kindness shown to their children. Time and again has it happened, in the history of Sabbath-school efforts, that worldly people, who never think of going to church themselves, and who would repel as intrusive any attempt directly to interfere with their own habits, are yet pleased with attention paid to their children by the faithful Sabbath-school teacher. Teachers in visiting such families on their errand of love, if wise and discreet in their work, are often greeted with unexpected kindness.

Sabbath-schools necessarily cost money. A large city school costs several hundred dollars in a year. The work of thorough exploration costs money. Though the work is done by voluntary, unpaid labour, there are always numerous incidental expenses. In certain parts of the field, as in destitute rural districts, and in pioneer regions, and wherever the institution has never yet been established, a paid agency must be employed, just as much as in undertaking to convert the heathen. If the Sabbath-school workers determine to make thorough work in their field, so that not a child shall be left uncared for, it must needs take no small amount of money. When such workers come together, to deliberate whether to go forward, the question, how shall the necessary funds be obtained, is often the lion in the path. So many objects are already pulling at the purse-strings of benevolence, that teachers fear to put in a new claim. Yet a fair trial always shows the difficulty to be unreal. For no cause is it so easy to raise money as for the Sabbath-school. It is a cause which comes right home to every hearthstone. After people have given to every other benevolent object, and the fountain of benevolence seems fairly exhausted, there is generally something still left for the cause of the little ones. Besides, there is always quite a number of persons, not in the habit of giving to any other cause, who will give cheerfully and liberally to this.

IX.

WORKING ALONE AND WORKING TOGETHER.

If one were in want of a new classification of men, it would not be difficult to divide them according to their different modes of doing things. Two modes of action especially have so many adherents that almost all mankind would fall into one class or the other. These modes may be called, for convenience, the solitary and the social. One man desires to conduct his affairs, even those of a benevolent kind, entirely by himself, consulting nobody, copying nobody, interfering with nobody, working away in his own little enclosure of the great vineyard, a solitary, unconnected unit. Another man is just the opposite. Nothing interests him, unless as a part of some concerted, associated scheme. He seems to think that it would be wasting his energies, were he to put them forth in solitary effort. He would fain do good in the mass, and by the wholesale. He must always have some great plan afloat. He can do nothing without getting up a society for it.

These two modes of acting are often seen in the Sabbath-school effort. One teacher is unwearied in the instruction of his class. He is never absent. He makes diligent preparation for his lesson. He is always punctual. He is faithful in visiting. He knows the social, domestic, moral, and intellectual wants of his scholars, and is faithful and persevering in trying to supply them. His own little plot of the garden is always green and fruitful. His own class is a model and an ornament to the school. So far it is well. But he seems to forget that he has other duties. He practically ignores the fact that he owes something to the school at large. So far as other classes or the general interests of the school are concerned, he feels that he has done all that is required of him, so long as neither he nor his class disturb anybody else. There is even in his benevolence a lurking selfishness. His conduct plainly says, "Am I my brother's keeper?"

Sometimes the disposition referred to does not take this extreme type. The teacher is interested not only in his own class, but in the whole school. He wishes and works to make the whole school prosperous. But it is only *his* school, or the church school. His thoughts and his cares go not beyond that boundary. It is still only an enlarged selfishness. If his school, or the school of his church prospers, he is satisfied. His conscience is at peace. Why should he trouble himself because the mission-school does not get along well? Why should he be troubled because one-half the entire youthful population goes to no school? Is he his brother's keeper? Is he responsible for the ignorance, and the neglect, and the ungodliness that everywhere abound? The duties to his own class are diligently performed. His own class and school are full and are well taught. What more can be expected of him?

These are the solitary workers. In the other extreme, you will find the teacher whose chief delight is to be in some great excitement, or at some big meeting. His heart warms towards brethren of other denominations. He is fond of visiting other schools. He never misses a convention. He goes in for general measures. The more wide-sweeping and comprehensive a plan, the better it suits him. But he does not like to trouble himself with details. He expects somehow to convert the world in the mass, by platform speeches, and societies. Solitary work, sitting down soberly and quietly to do any one single thing, of the thousand things that make up a grand scheme, is dull and stupid to him. He can expatiate fluently and eloquently upon the way to bring about some wonderful plan of benevolence, but he cannot keep his own school in order, he cannot keep his own class together. He is ready with his sympathies and his efforts for his fellow-labourers in the vineyard, but his own particular little plot of ground is overrun with weeds and thorns.

It is not my purpose to say which of these extremes is the most mischievous. The point I wish to make is that neither extreme is necessary. Platform-speaking and convention-going in themselves establish no schools, and teach no children, and save no souls. The first, main, indispensable work, without which all else is mere scaffolding, is the individual solitary work. But let not the teacher who does this work faithfully and conscientiously imagine that his duty as a teacher is ended. Let it never be forgotten that the Sabbath-school work is a mission-work. Its most important function is to gather in the outcast. It aims to reach the neglected. This work of aggression upon the outlying destitutions of society requires conference and co-operation.

I hold it, therefore, to be the interest and the duty of individual Sabbath-school workers, while not neglecting solitary work, to add their personal quota of service to every wise and prudent measure of concerted effort. I think that many teachers, most excellent and exemplary and faithful in other respects, come short in this. They rarely attend a meeting of the teachers of their school. Such persons not only fail in duty, but they miss a great privilege. The solitary worker is very apt to acquire contracted and imperfect notions on many subjects. The very best way to improve one's own methods is to mingle with others. This interchange of thought always suggests to the wide-awake teacher something new and better. Besides, by this friendly contact of differing minds, new energy and life are caught. The heart is warmed. Impulses are given and received that never would have been experienced in mere solitary work.

In order to the universal spread and diffusion of the Sabbath-school cause through any community, the individual workers in it should feel bound, not merely to do their own work diligently and well, in the teaching of their particular class and school, but to extend a helping hand to others, by friendly co-operation and counsel, by collecting and diffusing Sabbath-school intelligence, by going themselves or sending others into destitute neighbourhoods for the purpose of collecting the children who are out of school, and of conversing freely and kindly with their parents on the subject.

X.

THE LONG VACATION.

No practical question in the actual management of Sabbath-schools is more pressing than that of closing or not closing them in certain seasons of the year. Country schools, in many places, are closed all winter, that is, full one-half the year. City schools, in like manner, close in midsummer for about two months nominally. But as it takes at least a month, after opening in the fall, to get the stragglers all back, and as the children in the spring always begin to fall off in advance of the summer vacation, and in anticipation of it, the city school is suspended, so far as real efficiency is concerned, from three to four months, or about one-third of the year.

That this long periodical suspension of active service in the Sabbath-school is a serious evil, no one questions. We profess to believe that religion is immeasurably the greatest human concern, and that religious knowledge transcends in importance all other kinds of knowledge as much as eternity transcends time. Yet we require our children to pursue the knowledge of arithmetic, geography, grammar, and other similar branches, whose main bearing is upon their temporal interests, five days, or five and a half days in the week, and that, too, from five to six full hours a day in school, while for gaining religious knowledge they are virtually, in nine cases out of ten, limited to one single day, and on that day, in most schools, to one session of an hour and a half, and in many schools to a session of one hour. The average number of hours in a week, in the week-day school, given to the acquisition of secular knowledge, is thirty. The average given in the Sabbath-school, to the acquisition of Bible-knowledge, is less than two! Shall we increase this shocking disparity by suspending the Bible-school every year from one-third to one-half the year? I do verily believe, from no very limited observation, that the time occupied by the children of this country in the acquisition of secular knowledge, as compared with the time occupied in the acquisition of Bible-knowledge, is about in the proportion of fifty to one! Of course there are exceptions. There are families where Bible-study occupies a portion of time every day. There are schools where this rule holds. But these are few and far between; and for such as these, it matters not essentially whether the Sabbath-school is held at all or not. I am speaking here of the majority, the common mass of the children of the land, to whom practically the Sabbath-school is the only place and time for Bible-study; and for these, I say again, the disproportion between our professed estimate of the value of God's word and of religious truth, and the actual place we give it in our scheme of education, is utterly shocking.

I do not say that there is never, in any place, such a combination of circumstances that the Sabbath-school should not be suspended in summer or in winter. I would not judge my brethren. To their own Master they stand or fall. But surely, before closing any school, the teachers will do well to ponder the grave consideration presented above. Is the proportion of time now given to Bible-study by the young in any congregation so very considerable that the teachers can afford to fritter away a third or a half of it, except for the most imperative reasons?

It is difficult, without doubt, to keep a city school going in midsummer. Many of the teachers leave the city for health for a month or two. Many of the scholars also, belonging to families in easy circumstances, leave the city in midsummer. These facts necessarily break in seriously upon the regularity of the exercises. Still, the cases must be rare indeed, in which there do not remain, in any congregation, and in the hottest weather, scholars enough to form a considerable school, and teachers enough to take care of them. It is the custom of some superintendents to form a distinct organization of the school for the summer months. This is a great deal better than to disband the school entirely.

The suspension of Sabbath-schools in winter seems to have less shadow of reason for it than any custom with which I am acquainted of such general observance. For everything else, except the Bible, the winter is the chosen time for study. It is the time when there is most leisure in the community, and when the mental faculties are most vigorous, and take hold of study with most keenness. To give special point to the anomaly, the Sabbath-schools which are suspended in winter are mostly held in those very school-houses where the day-school can be kept up only in winter. Will not the teachers of schools, where this pernicious custom has prevailed, break in upon it, and make an effort to keep their schools open all the year round?

5 *

XI.

ATTENDANCE OF SABBATH-SCHOOL CHILDREN UPON CHURCH.

So far as I have been able to learn from the English religious papers, the children of the Sabbath-schools in England are required, sometimes compelled, to attend the church service. When the school closes, the classes move in a body into the church, with their teachers. This, we are led to believe, is almost the universal custom. Another fact, which we have upon the same authority, is that the great mass of these children, after arriving at adult age, cease their attendance upon church, and are lost sight of. They disappear entirely from all religious circles. It would seem as if the great majority of the Sabbath-school children in that country were of the poorer classes, such as in this country fill mainly our mission-schools. These children are brought in great numbers into the schools, and while there attend church, but at an early age, say thirteen or fourteen, they drop off both from school and church, and are heard of no more in connection with religious services or institutions. That is, the Sabbath-school does not succeed to the extent that its friends wish and aim, in bringing any considerable body of the population permanently into the Christian church.

There are of course many exceptions to this fact. It could not be otherwise from the very nature of the Sabbath-school. But that such has been the general result of Sabbath-school operations in England, seems to be admitted by the friends of the cause. Their children do not, as a general thing, grow up into a permanent part of the congregation. Many reasons have been assigned for this. The chief are these two. First, the services in the churches which they are compelled to attend, are distasteful to them. These services are adapted entirely to adults. They are as unintelligible to the children as if conducted in Hebrew or Latin. Secondly, the children, while in the church, are made as thoroughly uncomfortable as crowding, hard seats, and semi-suffocation can well make them. Of course, as soon as they are old enough to escape from parental restraint, and to act for themselves, they leave for ever a place which is to them a scene of no pleasant recollections.

Sabbath-schools in this country differ in many particulars from those in England. Yet they are not so unlike but that we may profit by the example of our English brethren. If we are rightly informed, there is not in our schools that sharp distinction between the children of the rich and the children of the poor, which exists in England. In our congregations, and especially in our schools, rich and poor mingle together more than they do in England. A larger portion of the scholars gathered into our schools remain in them to adult age, and become a permanent part of the congregation. So far as my own observation goes, the tendency of things is in this direction, and we are slowly but surely improving in this respect. In the schools, with which I have been personally connected, if the children of a family not attending any place of worship, were brought into the school, it was generally the precursor to bringing the family into the church. Various appliances, social and domestic, were brought to bear upon the point, and rarely without effect. Still we are far from accomplishing, by means of our Sabbath-schools, all that we might accomplish in the way of building up and replenishing our churches. The Sabbath-school is a broad net, and we draw in large numbers, undoubtedly. But, somehow, we let entirely too many slip through the meshes. If all the families represented in our Sabbath-schools, and especially all those in our mission-schools, could be secured to our congregations, and if all the children in our Sabbath-schools could be counted on as secured permanently to religious influences and institutions, there would be a growth and development of Christian churches such as we have not yet seen.

What are some of the things to be done towards the attainment of such a result?

In the first place, we should aim at it. Give no countenance to the idea that the Sabbath-school effort is an outside affair, to be managed and conducted apart from the church. It is rather the church, the people of God, exercising their Christian activity in that particular mode. The church has its Sabbath-school, as one of the means of training its own children in the doctrines and duties of religion. The children of the church attend the school, and then as a matter of course remain with their parents to attend public worship. This fact is a good basis of operations for inducing the other children of the school to attend. Let the teachers, and let the church authorities, keep this aim ever before their eyes. There is no way by which an irreligious family can be so surely and effectually benefited, as by inducing them to become connected with a Christian congregation and to attend statedly religious worship. Next to a house to shelter their bodies, a family should have some religious *home*, a place in some house of worship which they consider theirs, and in which they appear statedly on the Sabbath. There is no means so effectual for securing this end, as an efficient, well-ordered Sabbath-school. Teachers and superintendents should accustom themselves more than they now do, to regard this as an important, indeed a leading part of their work. The Sabbath-school is an immense network of influences, and it should be continually putting out its feelers in every direction, to see what can be done towards reaching and bringing in those families which are without any church connections.

I have never been in favour of compulsory measures to secure the attendance of the Sabbath-school children upon public worship. I have known schools, where at the close of school the outer door is locked, and the classes in a body are marched into the gallery, and every means, short of actual violence, is used to prevent straggling. The effect is uniformly bad. Let the children, whose parents attend, go and sit with their parents, and let the teachers endeavour by persuasion and argument to induce others to remain, whose parents do not attend. But do not require attendance, as a matter of authority.

The trustees of the church, or whoever have the ordering of the material arrangements, have much to do with securing the attendance of this class of children. These little ones need a kind of church accommodation which they rarely get. They need comfortable seats. If the big people, who have the ordering of such matters, could be compelled to sit for a few Sabbaths as the children do, on seats so wide that their backs can get no support except by a painful curvature of the spine, and so high that their feet can by no possibility reach the floor, and their legs must by necessity hang dangling in the air, they would appreciate better the dislike which children often acquire against going to church. The same child who sits with pleased delight on his snug, low bench in the school-room, runs with aversion from that cruel perch to which the church people assign him. Will not our church builders and church furnishers acquire a little common sense? If you want children to attend church, and to love so to do, you must make it comfortable for them. They must have seats in church, as they do in their homes, suited to the size of their bodies and the length of their limbs. Such of them, too, as sit by themselves, instead of being thrust afar off into some remote corner of the gallery, as far as possible from the minister, should be brought close beneath the notice of his kindling eye and his winning smile. Children, beyond all others, are moved by sympathy. Our Saviour did not place them on the outer and most remote circle of his congregations, but placed them in the midst, close to his person, and took them in his arms. A certain minister of a country church, actually had small, low benches placed for the children in the open space just in front of his pulpit, and not only so, but he let them fill the pulpit steps. The consequence was, the little ones thronged with delight to his church, and their parents followed them, and in a few months his congregation more than doubled.

But it is in vain to entice children to church unless you have something for them to hear or to do after they are there. Let any one ask himself, after attending almost any church service, certainly any five out of six, what has there been in this long session of an hour and a half or two hours, to interest the attention of a child? The singing has been either so scientific or so grum that no child, at least, could enter into it with any emotion. Seldom does he hear either a prayer for him specifically, or a prayer into which he as a child can enter. The sermons, like the rest of the services, are above his range. The minister not only never preaches specially to the children, but he never, while distributing the bread of life to the grown folks, pauses to drop a few crumbs here and there to the little ones. Why could not a clergyman, sometimes, break in upon this chilling routine of the sermon, and after having set forth some portion of doctrine for the benefit of the seniors, pause for a moment and say, "Children, this applies to you too, and I will now show you how?" How the young, and the old too, would wake up at such an announcement! Christian ministers, if you want your young people to cleave to you, and to love your ministrations, and not to wander off into other folds, see that you let no Sabbath pass without giving them some kindly word of recognition. Let no sermon be considered complete which does not contain at least one paragraph of warning or encouragement for the young, and so written and spoken as to be within the comprehension of even the youngest. Let there be no child in your audience who shall not, at some time, have occasion to feel, "My minister must have been thinking of me when he said that." All ministers have not the gift that some have, of talking to the young. But if any minister really has the young substantially and habitually in his thoughts and on his heart, he will find expression for his emotions, and the children of his congregation will feel that they have some real interest in being in the house of God.

Sabbath-school teachers should aim to secure the stated attendance of their children upon the services of the sanctuary; to this end, it is important that the pastor, in conducting the services, have something in every service suited to the wants and capacities of the young, and also that the authorities of the church have such arrangements for the seating of the little folks while in the house of God as to make it comfortable and pleasant to them.

XII.

HOW TO KEEP THE OLDER SCHOLARS.

Of the vexed questions which occupy the thoughts of teachers and superintendents, when gathered in convention, none is more directly practical, or more frequently discussed, than the question, how shall we retain the big boys and girls?

The man must be lacking in the first element of wisdom, who should undertake to be oracular on such a subject. Yet, it is obvious, from the example of many schools, that the thing required, *may* be done. In many places, it is done. It is what the French call a fact accomplished. I have seen schools, I have laboured in schools, where it was difficult, by mere inspection, to distinguish between the school and the congregation, between the scholars and the teachers. There seemed a regular gradation, from the little ones in the infant class, just beginning to say "Who made you?" and to sing "There is a Happy Land," all the way up through the junior classes, the classes of young men and young women and the adult Bible-classes, to those of gray hairs and tottering steps. It was not easy to say, when school broke up, which were scholars, which were teachers. The Sabbath-school was to a great extent the congregation, only organized in squads and companies, instead of being in one compact regiment. In such a congregation, it was evident that the duty of studying God's word was not thought to be confined to the young, nor indeed to any class, but as being incumbent on all.

I have seen other schools, where quite a different state of things existed. In going into such a school, it is obvious on mere inspection, that it is a school for *children*, and for quite young children too. If a young man or young woman, conscious of deficiency and desirous of improvement, should wish to join such a school, or to remain in it, he or she would feel out of place. In such a school, the children expect, as a matter of course, to leave school, when they are twelve, or at the most fourteen years of age. They begin to thin out at ten, and by fourteen they are all gone. No power seems able to arrest the torrent of desertion in a school where such a state of things is once established.

Were I called upon to labour in such a field I would not begin by railing at the big boys and girls, much less by trying to bribe them to remain by extra inducements in the shape of premiums and excursions. Nor would I persuade their parents to compel an unwilling and sullen attendance by bare authority. After doing what I could to make the school-room comfortable and attractive, in the way of light, air, heat, and agreeable sights and sounds, I would set myself to work to induce the oldest and most dignified and respectable persons in the congregation to join the school, not as teachers, but as *scholars.* I have faith to believe that there are few congregations where a discreet, sober-minded superintendent, by presenting this subject personally and privately to some of the leading men and women past middle-age, might not meet with success. There are pious old ladies in every congregation, those who with hymn-book in hand are always seen at the weekly prayer-meeting, who would be glad to come together on the Sabbath to read and talk together over God's word under the guidance of some competent instructor. Let the superintendent who wishes to prevent the big boys and girls from straying, begin by forming, if possible, a class of grandmothers and a class of grandfathers, and so work his way down. When he gets some of the grandfathers and grandmothers in school, and then some of the fathers and mothers, and then some of the young men and women, he will find no difficulty with the boys and girls.

The most successful experiment I ever knew, in the way of establishing a school, began in this wise. First a superintendent was chosen, before there was any school to superintend. There was a schoolroom and a superintendent, but neither scholars nor teachers. The first step was the formation of two adult Bible-classes, one of gentlemen, all married, who met in the morning, the other of ladies, all married but two or three, who met in the afternoon. Younger persons and children came in gradually, as the superintendent was prepared for them. In that school, the idea of leaving it, or of declining to enter it, on account of being too old, has never had a footing.

In the matter of our Sabbath-schools, we are influenced too much by the analogy of the week-day school. Every child who goes to the week-day school expects, as a matter of course, to leave it sooner or later. There is a certain amount of secular knowledge which his parents desire and intend him to acquire, and then his school-days are ended. Those studying for the professions remain longer. Even they, however, have a limit to their school and college attendance. But in the study of God's word, we should know no limit. We may study it until we are eighty, and yet be but babes in divine knowledge. Here we must be always learners. We should be always students. True, we may continue our studies solitarily. But there is an impulse given to study by the social element of our nature, which we are most unwise not to profit by. A half a dozen or a dozen minds of kindred age and sympathies, studying together, are kindled by the contact, and make progress in knowledge never reached by solitary study.

The Sabbath-school, indeed, is that one institution from which there is and there should be no diploma of *graduation*, unless it be that of Simeon, "Now lettest thou thy servant depart in peace." With the exception of those prevented by sickness and unavoidable duties elsewhere, the school properly and legitimately consists of the entire congregation, from the infants to the grandfathers and the grandmothers. As we are never too young to begin to learn, so we are never too old or too wise to continue the study of God's word; and when we shall have generally in our schools more frequent examples of the old people's classes, or "spectacle classes," to be found in some schools, we shall hear less of the difficulty of retaining the older boys and girls.

XIII.

GRADED SABBATH-SCHOOLS.

Nearly all the substantial improvements which have been made in the week-day schools, have their root in a proper system of grading the schools, that is, in having them so arranged, into higher and lower schools, that scholars who are in the same stage of advancement may recite together. A proper system of classification secures for a school what a proper sub-division of labour secures in mechanical occupations. In mechanical and material pursuits, the more minute and exact the sub-division of labour, the more perfect will be the product, and at the same time the more economical. In like manner, the more complete the classification you can make in any school, the cheaper will be the instruction and the better its quality. The quality rises, as the rate of cost falls.

Nor is there any mystery about this. Let a teacher have, say, thirty scholars. Now if these are all in different stages of advancement, if one is learning the alphabet, and another is in easy readings, and a third is beginning to study geography, and a fourth grammar, and so on, all the way up to the higher branches, so that no two or three of the children can recite together, it is obvious that the teacher's time, broken up into infinitesimal portions, cannot be made of much practical value to any one. Each scholar will get on the average about two minutes an hour of the teacher's time. If, on the other hand, all the scholars are in precisely the same stage of advancement, if they are all working on the same rule in arithmetic, have the same lesson in grammar, are in the same part of geography, and of whatever other lesson they may have, the teacher's whole time is substantially given to every scholar. Whatever explanation or instruction is given to one, is given to all. Under such circumstances, skilled teaching can show its full power, and scholars will improve apace, and at a rate of progress not possible under any other conditions.

A moderate number of scholars, perfectly classified, and studying together under one skilled teacher, will improve more rapidly than they would if each individual scholar had a teacher wholly to himself, for there will be the stimulus of competition and of the social impulse. Solitary study, under a private tutor, is a dull business to a child. The lesson which is soporific or repulsive, as a solitary exercise, becomes a delight when learned in company. As with learning, so with teaching. It is a dull, mind-benumbing business to teach one child. That the mind of the teacher may be roused to its highest and best exertions, the stimulus of numbers is needed. In every aspect of the case, therefore, good classification in school is an indispensable element of success. Indeed, it is no exaggeration to say that a class of thirty scholars of exactly equal attainments would be brought forward as rapidly by a single teacher, as the same number would be by thirty teachers, if the class was so ill assorted that every scholar had to have a separate lesson. The efficiency and the commercial value of the one teacher in such a case, would be multiplied thirty-fold.

Cannot something be done towards attaining like results in our Sabbath-schools? Very many superintendents and pastors, I know, have the subject often in their thoughts. But the way seems hedged up. Indeed, the difficulties are great, and well-nigh insurmountable. Yet so great a benefit should not be lightly abandoned.

The first and indeed the indispensable requisite, in any really efficient gradation in a Sabbath-school, is that the school should be a large one. The larger the number that comes under one organization, the more perfect the classification can be made. This is the secret of the complete classification which is reached in the public schools of our large cities. From the lowest division in a Primary School up to the highest division in the High School, there are more than twenty distinct, well-defined stages of advancement, representing in fact so many successive schools, rising one above another in regular order and progression. But in accomplishing this result, it should be remembered, the organization embraces some fifty or sixty thousand children. The Sabbath-school of a single church can never be sufficiently numerous to secure a classification so complete as this. Yet with an attendance of three or four hundred, which many of our city schools have, a gradation might be accomplished of a very efficient character.

Were it left to me to propose an organization for such a school, and the proper means were placed at my disposal, I would begin by assorting the scholars into three portions. The first portion, consisting of those who cannot read, would constitute the Primary department. They should be kept in that department until they could read sufficiently to be able to study lessons by themselves from a book. The third portion of the school should consist of adults and of those who are already well advanced in biblical knowledge, and should constitute a Senior department. All between these two portions would form an Intermediate department, and would constitute the main school. In a school of three hundred, there might be, say, fifty in the Primary or Infant class, fifty in the Senior department, and two hundred in the Intermediate or main school.

The Primary or Infant class might in the main all have the same lesson. They should have, besides one principal teacher, several assistant teachers, not less than one for every ten or twelve, each assistant being charged with a certain section of the class, to carry out into detail to each scholar the instructions of the principal teacher.

The classes constituting the Senior department might, under competent teachers, be left comparatively independent in their selection of courses of study. The classification in this department would be made mainly with reference to age, sex, social position, personal friendships and affinities, and the like. A class, organized on these grounds, under the direction and with the concurrence of the superintendent, would take up some book of Scripture, or some other special study, sufficient to occupy them for a season, and having completed it, would then take up some other subject of inquiry.

But, between the Primary department and the Senior department of the school, there should be a regular course of Scriptural study, running through not less than four or five years. In other words, the Intermediate or Main school should be divided into four or five stages, and for each stage there should be a distinct course of study sufficient to occupy the Sabbaths for one entire year. For each of these divisions of the main school, consisting of forty or fifty scholars, all having the same lessons, there should be one principal teacher, aided by assistant teachers, not less than one for every ten or twelve scholars. The scholars should be grouped into sections of ten or twelve, each section with an assistant teacher, who should carry out the details of instruction, but the whole forty or fifty should in other respects be considered and treated as one class. The time for instruction and recitation should be divided about equally between the principal teacher and the assistant teachers. Supposing the time for instruction to be one hour, the principal teacher would ordinarily occupy ten minutes in the beginning in general explanations, then give the assistants thirty minutes to go over the lesson in detail with their several sections, and then the principal teacher would occupy twenty minutes with the whole class. While the principal teacher was occupying the whole class, the assistant teachers should each see to the individual scholars of his Section for the purpose of securing attention and quiet.

In order to give such an organization of a Sabbath-school proper efficiency there must be suitable accommodations in the way of rooms. Not only must there be a separate room for the Primary department, (which is now universally conceded,) but there must be a separate room for each of the five divisions of the Intermediate department. This is indispensable. It would be desirable also that each class in the Senior department should have a room to itself. But this is not indispensable. They might all occupy one room, but it should be separated entirely from the main school.

A mere glance at this plan will show that at least six skilled (if possible, professional) teachers would be needed, namely, one for the Primary or Infant department, and one for each division of the Intermediate department. Ordinary teachers, such as we have in all our Sabbath-schools, would do for the assistants. But the principal teachers must be of a superior grade. They must be persons who really know how to teach, and who have been accustomed to handle large classes. Under such teachers the assistants would rapidly improve in the matter of teaching, and would themselves soon become experts.

Perhaps it may make this plan clearer if I spread it out in a little different shape. It will be understood of course that the figures here used are assumed merely for convenience of illustration. In actual practice, no school can ever be thus rounded off into even figures. Some classes will have only four or five scholars, while others will have twelve or fifteen. The even numbers here given, or any others that might be assumed, serve to show the point towards which the organization is directed.

I. SENIOR DEPARTMENT, 50 scholars; II. MAIN SCHOOL, 200 scholars; III. INFANT SCHOOL, 50 scholars. Total, 300.

I.
SENIOR DEPARTMENT,
50 *Scholars.*

Class I.   1 teacher and 10 scholars.
Class II. 1 teacher and 10 scholars.
Class III. 1 teacher and 10 scholars.
Class IV. 1 teacher and 10 scholars.
Class V.   1 teacher and 10 scholars.

II.
MAIN SCHOOL.
200 Scholars.

DIVISION I. 1 PRINCIPAL TEACHER and 50 scholars.
    Class I.   1 assistant and 10 scholars.
    Class II. 1 assistant and 10 scholars.
    Class III. 1 assistant and 10 scholars.
    Class IV. 1 assistant and 10 scholars.
    Class V.   1 assistant and 10 scholars.

DIVISION II. 1 PRINCIPAL TEACHER and 50 scholars.
    Class I.   1 assistant and 10 scholars.
    Class II. 1 assistant and 10 scholars.
    Class III. 1 assistant and 10 scholars.
    Class IV. 1 assistant and 10 scholars.
    Class V.   1 assistant and 10 scholars.

DIVISION III. 1 PRINCIPAL TEACHER and 50 scholars.
    Class I.   1 assistant and 10 scholars.
    Class II. 1 assistant and 10 scholars.
    Class III. 1 assistant and 10 scholars.
    Class IV. 1 assistant and 10 scholars.
    Class V.   1 assistant and 10 scholars.

DIVISION IV. 1 PRINCIPAL TEACHER and 50 scholars.
    Class 1.   1 assistant and 10 scholars.
    Class II. 1 assistant and 10 scholars.
    Class III. 1 assistant and 10 scholars,

Class IV.   1 assistant and 10 scholars.
Class V.   1 assistant and 10 scholars.

III.
PRIMARY DEPARTMENT.
50 *Scholars*, 1 Principal Teacher.

Class I.   1 assistant and 10 scholars.
Class II.   1 assistant and 10 scholars.
Class III. 1 assistant and 10 scholars.
Class IV.   1 assistant and 10 scholars.
Class V.   1 assistant and 10 scholars.

A bare inspection of this programme will enforce, better than any argument could, certain necessary changes in our Sabbath-school arrangements.

1. We must have a different method of building from that which now prevails. There must be more rooms than we now have. In such a school as we have supposed, there must be at least six separate rooms, namely, one for the Senior Department, one for the Primary school, and one for each of the four Divisions of the Main school.

2. We must have in such a school at least five accomplished, thoroughly qualified teachers, namely, one as Principal teacher of the Primary or Infant school, and one for each of the four Divisions of the Main school.

3. From the Primary or Infant school up to the highest Division in the Main school, there should be an established and consecutive course of study. If a child grows up in the school from infancy, he

should go up regularly, class by class, until he has completed the full course, when he should be admitted into one of the adult classes forming the Senior Department. If a child is brought into the school from some other school, he should be placed in some one of the Divisions, according to his attainments and age, and advance from that point with the others.

4. All scholars in any one Division should have the same text-book and the same lesson.

5. The text-book for each Division should be such as could be completed in one year. This would make a four or five years' course for the Main school.

6. In each Division of the Main school, and also in the Infant school, the *instruction* would be given chiefly by the Principal teacher. He would give the comments and explanations. It would rest upon the Assistants to sit with their classes and keep the scholars in order and attentive while the Principal teacher was talking; to question each child in detail for the purpose of seeing whether the explanations of the Principal teacher had been understood; to hear each child answer the questions given to be answered, and recite the verses and hymns given to be committed to memory; to register the attendance; to attend to library books and papers, and to the collections; to hunt up, during the week, all absentees; and to report to the Principal teacher all cases of every kind requiring special attention.

7. No child should advance from the Primary or Infant school until (1.) it can read, and (2.) it is well grounded in certain rudiments of Christian doctrine, knowing thoroughly by memory the Lord's Prayer, the Ten Commandments, and the Apostles' Creed.

8. The Senior Department should be one from which there should be *no graduation*. The classes should be formed according to age, and elective affinity. Each class should pursue its own course, without any necessary connection with the other classes, and taking every year some new study sufficient to last through the year. There is no danger of their ever exhausting the subject of study which the Bible will furnish. The Senior Department will furnish the general reserve corps, from which teachers are to be drawn, either for temporary vacancies, or for regular service; and to this corps teachers should *return*, whenever they become disabled for active service.

Cannot *some* of these ideas be realized?

XIV.

CHURCH ARCHITECTURE AND SABBATH-SCHOOLS.

It is a gratifying fact, that of late years, when a church is to be built, the architect and the building committee assume that in their plans some provision is to be made for the Sabbath-school. This fact is significant. It shows that the Sabbath-school, as an institution of the church, is making steady growth. There is no surer sign of the progress of any idea, than its showing itself in solid brick and mortar. If one could collect drawings of all the churches built in the United States, say from 1800 to 1864, and arrange them in chronological order, according to the dates of their construction, he would have before him a striking exhibition, not only of Sabbath-school growth, but of the growth of many other ideas.

In this matter, there have been some large strides in the right direction, in the last five years. Some of the churches of the most recent construction, not only have a large and commodious school-room for the main school, but convenient class-rooms for Bible-classes, and a room separate from all others for the infant-school. Nor are these rooms thrust away into some dark corner, or down into some unwholesome cellar, but are as light, and airy, and pleasant in all respects, as the main hall of audience for the worship of the congregation.

Still there is room for improvement, and architects, who are mainly responsible for the enormous sins that have been committed in the matter of church-building, would do well, as a part of their professional study, to make themselves acquainted with the actual wants of the Sabbath-school. The younger part of a congregation, those who form the Sabbath-school, are always more numerous than the adults. Yet of the gross number of cubic feet enclosed within the church edifice, four-fifths will be devoted to the use of the room where the adults assemble for worship, while the remaining one-fifth will be counted ample for the uses of the schools.

This matter will never be on a right basis until it is accepted, as a starting point in erecting a church, that the schools should occupy at least one-half the entire cubic space of the structure, and cause at least one-half the entire expense. Let a building committee give that as one of the conditions of the house to be erected, and they will then begin to receive plans more in accordance with the real wants of a congregation. There will be fewer big steeples, perhaps, and fewer overgrown halls of audience, never half-filled. But there will also be fewer *pens* where human cattle, because they are children, are huddled together in violation of all the laws of health. A Sabbath-school in a large congregation wants the following things. First, a series of large rooms for its Main school. Secondly, one large room, or a series of moderate sized rooms, for the Senior classes. Thirdly, an Infant school-room.

The Primary or Infant-school is for those who cannot read, and who must be taught orally. Children of this age are soured and fretted, if confined to the quiet necessary in the main school. They are restless. They *ought* to have motion and noise. Long continued stillness and silence forced upon such children are a cruelty. Reciting in concert, interspersed with singing, and regulated bodily movements, are absolutely essential to their proper improvement. But these things require that they should have a room to themselves, where their movements and noise would not disturb others.

Suitable architectural arrangements, such as those here indicated, have a prodigious effect in building up a congregation. The material structure has much to do both in helping and hindering the spiritual edifice. Much of the church extension of late years has been by colonization. Families leave an old and well-filled church, not from disaffection, but for the purpose of forming a new church. Such a colony is in many respects like a new married couple preparing to begin housekeeping. Unfortunately, these new churches too often make the mistake of those young housekeepers, who do their best to build a dwelling-house all parlour, forgetting that the main comfort of a family depends upon the size and conveniences of the kitchen and the back buildings.

The most common mistake in constructing infant-school rooms is making them too small and with too low ceilings. Because the bodies of these little ones are diminutive and a great many of them can be seated in a room of moderate dimensions, it is therefore assumed that they do not need any more space. Architects forget that children have lungs, and that the lungs of a hundred children will vitiate the air of a room almost as fast as the lungs of a hundred adults, certainly faster than the lungs of fifty adults. Yet one hundred little children will, without the slightest compunction, be thrust into a room, and kept there for one or two hours, where twenty grown persons would never think of staying. The infant-school room ought to have as high a ceiling as any other part of the school. In addition to this, the mode of seating the children by a raised gallery places them so compactly, and accommodates so many in so small a space, that at least four times as much unoccupied space should be left in other parts of the room, to prevent the evil effects of over-crowding. Special care should be taken also that there be some outlet for the foul air from the upper part of these raised galleries. If the church architect could be compelled to sit for the last half hour of the school session upon the upper tier of one of these raised galleries, and receive the exhalations from a hundred pair of lungs, each having breathed over for the hundredth time substantially the same volume of fetid air, he would probably get some new ideas in regard to the practical wants for which his professional skill was invoked.

If school architects could once get some right ideas on this subject, there would be less difficulty in the way of improving our Sabbath-schools. The greatest and most urgent want of our schools at this time is suitable classification. Many teachers and superintendents are fully alive to the subject. But, alas! the material obstacles are invincible. A general separation of our large congregational schools into different departments, such as that which obtains in our public week-day schools, would be of the greatest possible advantage. But with the material accommodations afforded by our present mode of church-building, the thing is impossible.

XV.

INFANT-SCHOOLS.

The importance of the infant department of the Sabbath-school is generally conceded. No Sabbath-school is now considered complete, which does not include an Infant class. This part of the school is important, not only because Christians wish in the earliest stage of childhood to pre-occupy the young mind and heart with religious knowledge, but also because the Infant-school is the great feeder of the Main school. The main school draws its chief supplies of recruits from this source.

The great want of the Infant-school is suitable teachers. No department of the whole Sabbath-school work, not even that of the superintendent, requires such peculiar talent. Other positions in the Sabbath-school may require greater talent, or more varied knowledge; but none requires gifts so peculiar. There is a special style of heart, mind, and manner, needed for the one who would teach an Infant-class. No other gifts can be taken as a substitute for these. It must be these or nothing.

Most of our Infant-school teachers are ladies. But the gift for this work is not confined to that sex, nor is it confined to young persons. I have never seen young children more interested nor more thoroughly excited, than by Dr. Archibald Alexander, of Princeton. Some of the very best specimens of Infant teaching that I have seen have been by gentlemen. Still, in a majority of cases, as a matter of fact, our infant teachers are ladies, and, as a general thing, teachers belonging to that sex have greater aptitude for the service than men.

To teach the Infant-school requires in the first place great vivacity of manner. The teacher must be full of life, ready of utterance, and rapid in motion. The knowledge to be communicated must be all at the tip of the tongue. There is no time, in the infant-class, for slow elaboration of thought, for long circumlocutions, or ponderous abstractions. The knowledge must be all sorted, parcelled out, and ready for instantaneous delivery. A lively imagination is indispensable. A streak of quiet humour does not come amiss. All children are born humourists. All children also are instinctively dramatic. A good infant teacher must be a good story-teller, and ought to be something of an actor. Things must be pictured out, so that they can be vividly realized by the imagination. The eyes and the hands of the teacher must be as active as the tongue. No part of the person indeed can be idle. Sitting down is out of the question. Using a text-book is equally denied. The teacher must be all the while on her feet, all the while in motion, hearing everything, seeing every one, ready to start something new the instant another matter is ended, never at a loss for a story, or a good Bible verse, with a heart full of love, and a voice full of melody, and if possible with that pleasant, sunshiny face that goes so directly to the child's heart. Above all things, the infant teacher must be a good SINGER.

God seems to have gifted a certain proportion of his people with the qualities necessary for this peculiar service, as if on purpose that his little ones might not be neglected. Bezaleel and Aholiab were no more definitely gifted by nature for their peculiar work on the construction of the tabernacle than are persons for the work of teaching the little ones. I never yet have been connected with a congregation,—and I have been connected with many,—in which I did not know some persons in whom the possession of these gifts might be discovered. It is one of the duties of the superintendent and of the pastor to be on the look-out for persons who have this skill, and to bring it out into active exercise. I believe that a great deal of unemployed talent of this kind is lying dormant in the church.

A raised platform, or gallery, for seating the children, is indispensable to a good infant-school. The children must be all seated so that every child can see the teacher, and the teacher see every child. They ought also to sit rather compactly, especially if the class be large. There should be likewise partitions between the seats, so that each child will occupy just so much space. The object of this is, partly to prevent them from crowding each other, but mainly to give to the class when seated that orderly and symmetrical appearance in which the little ones themselves so much delight. To promote this end still farther, the teacher should never allow them to sit scattered about the room in a straggling manner. The vacant seats should be all filled. If there are sixty seats and only forty children present, let these forty be seated compactly and symmetrically, with no gaps between. Care in this matter not only helps the teacher in keeping them in concert in their movements of every kind, but it has a wonderful effect upon the children themselves. Nothing pleases children more than an appearance of snugness, and cosiness, and order.

Concerted action is indispensable in the Infant-school. They sing together, pray together, recite together, and in all things act as one. This mode of recitation is particularly valuable for the kind of lessons which are peculiarly appropriate to that age. Their business is to store the memory with texts of Scripture, hymns, catechisms, and other forms of good words. The volume of sound growing out of the united voices of fifty or a hundred children, all speaking in measured utterance, precisely the same words, powerfully impresses the memory, and children learn a great deal in that way with very little labour.

Young children, like all other young animals, are

by nature restless and fidgety, and like to make a noise. It is possible, indeed, by a system of vigorous and harsh repression, to restrain this restlessness, and to keep these little ones for an hour or more in such a state of decorous primness as not to molest weak nerves. But such a system of forced constraint is not natural to children, any more than to lambs or to kittens, and it is not a wise method of teaching, either for the Sabbath-school or the week-day school. Let the youngsters make a noise, only let it be noise of the right kind, and duly regulated. Let them exercise, not only their lungs, but also their limbs, moving in concert, rising up, sitting down, turning round, raising their hands, pointing to objects to which their attention is called, looking at objects which are shown to them. Movement and noise are the life of a child. In school they should be regulated, but not repressed. To make young children sit perfectly still, and keep perfect silence, for any considerable length of time, is next door to murder. I do verily believe that it sometimes is murder. The health, and often the lives of these little ones are sacrificed to a false theory, drawn from our ideas of what is decorous in grown folks. There is no occasion to torture a child, in order to teach it. God did not so mean it. Only let our teaching be in accordance with the wants of his young nature, and the school-room will be to the child the happiest and most attractive spot on earth.

XVI.

THE USE OF BOOKS IN INFANT-SCHOOLS.

INFANT-SCHOOLS are for children who cannot read, and who must be taught altogether orally. It may seem strange to some that books should be wanted for such schools, except, perhaps, a manual or two for the teacher. Indeed, in many Infant-schools which I have visited, there were no indications of a library, or of books being used in any way. I think this is a serious mistake. Though children cannot read, they love dearly to be read to, and the writers and publishers of children's books have employed their energies largely in the production of just this sort of books, namely, books to be read to the young. I hold it to be even more important for the infant-scholar to take home a library book, than for the older scholars to do so. A book taken by an older scholar is usually read in silence and read by him alone. But the book taken by the infant-scholar is carried to the father or mother, or to some other member of the family, to be read aloud to the little one. Often indeed on the Sabbath evening, especially in the poorer class of families, the father takes the little one on his knee and reads aloud to him the tiny volume brought from the school. Not only the father and the child thus get the benefit of its teachings, but frequently the whole family group cluster around in rapt attention, and drink in its precious truths. Moreover, the truths thus simplified and brought down to the capacity of a child, often have a strange power over the feelings and consciences of adults, beyond that of truth presented in the ordinary way. There are on record numerous instances of persons who had grown old in impenitence, being brought to serious reflection by reading children's books and papers. That class of people whose children chiefly fill our mission-schools, are often interested in religious subjects by means of the books brought home by their children, particularly by those brought by the young children who cannot read, and whose books must be read to them.

In order, however, that the infants' library may be thus useful, some care must be taken in the selection of the books. A book is not necessarily suited to this purpose, because it is a small book, or because it has pretty pictures, or a showy exterior, or because it abounds in that stuff, equally nauseous to children and to grown folks, usually called "baby-talk." The point needed, in order to interest the children, is that the matter itself be really interesting, and then that it be simple. But this simplicity is in no way dependent on that ridiculous and abominable jargon which has been referred to. Too many of the so-called "Libraries," whether for the infants or for older children, are mere receptacles for rubbish that could not otherwise be disposed of. These "Libraries" always contain *some* good books. But for every real good, live book, thus put into uniform binding, in order to make a "Library," the credulous purchaser usually has thrust upon him at least two that are of no conceivable use except to fill out the complement of volumes needed. In purchasing books for any kind of library, beware of this mischievous idea of uniformity of size and binding. Buy a good book, that is, a book with the right kind of reading in it, wherever you can find it, and whatever its shape or colour, or style of binding, only avoiding styles that are unusually expensive, or that otherwise have something positively objectionable. Many a library has been killed by the ridiculous desire to have its shelves look like a smooth, rectangular piece of brick-work. Children shrink instinctively from these prim, faultless specimens of book-binder's cabinet-work. They know too well that there is not the place to look for pretty stories.

I repeat, then, if the superintendent of an Infant-school expects to accomplish much by his library, he must first take some pains in the selection of his books. Seventy-five or a hundred volumes, each chosen intelligently, because of its own independent merits, are worth more than a thousand volumes collected by the usual omnium-gatherum process.

Among the thousand, there may be, and probably are, more than a hundred that are really good. But the children in the Infant-school have no power of choice, and have to take the books just as they come, good, bad, or indifferent. It is therefore doubly needful to see that no book finds its way into this collection which will not reward the expectant little one that fondly takes it home in the hope of a treat.

XVII.

MUSIC IN SABBATH-SCHOOLS.

In nothing, probably, has there been a greater change in Sabbath-schools than in the music. I refer not merely to the character and style of the music used, but to the position it holds, and the importance attached to it, as one of the essential and potent agencies of the institution in accomplishing its beneficent results. I recollect well the first Sabbath-school I ever attended, and the grim and ponderous tune to which we youngsters were solemnly exhorted to trail our voices, while a hymn of equally unattractive character dragged its slow length along. The singing was a religious duty, to which we were expected to give heed, and which we tried faithfully to discharge, as we would have tried to submit cheerfully to an amputation, had circumstances required it, or as we would have walked to the school, if necessary, barefoot through the snow, as one boy actually did rather than forego its privileges. Yes! the singing of the hymns was a solemn part of the programme, to be gone through with without flinching. But as an expression of gladness, as an act of devout joy, as a service, the mere announcement of which should awaken all over the school anticipations of lively delight, the thing was unknown. This was altogether a discovery of a later day, the full knowledge and appreciation of which have not even yet reached many schools.

In speaking of Infant-schools, I referred to the physical activity of the young, and the necessity of adapting our school exercises to the wants of their nature. The same idea should govern us in the selection of school music. The music suited to persons advanced in life is no more suited to children, than would be the measured and solemn gait of these aged persons. Childhood is jubilant and quick in its emotions. The lively treble of its voice is only an index of the soul that speaks through it. If music is really to take hold of the feelings of children, it must, in the first place, be simple. But, next to this, and paramount above every other quality, it must be quick and lively in its general movement. It is not necessary, however, to this life and simplicity, that the music should be trifling. I have seen schools where, in the attempt to avoid humdrum, the music had run into the opposite extreme, and had degenerated into mere slang. There is in some tunes a measure of softness and gentleness, in which children greatly delight, and which is perfectly compatible with liveliness. It is impossible to look over a congregation of children singing a tune of this kind, and not read in their faces an expression of lively and yet subdued pleasure, as far removed on the one side, from the noisy turbulence sometimes seen, as from the dull, lifeless, dragging monotony often seen on the other. Children will indeed join in with this noisy vociferation. It is easy, and they rather like it. But it does not give them that inward satisfaction and pleasure which they derive from singing tunes where the predominant expression is that of gentleness and sweetness, combined with a lively movement of the voice.

Nor is it necessary, in order to make the music attractive to children, that the words should be unmeaning doggerel, or that they should be low and trifling, or that they should be flippant and profane. Children undoubtedly will sing such pieces with great gusto. But the superintendent who allows their minds and their tastes to be debauched with such trash, does a great wrong. A great deal of music is sung in our Sabbath-schools that may be very fit for a pic-nic, or for the circus, but that has no business in the Sabbath-school, and is utterly unsuited for a religious service. The words, equally with the music, may be cheerful, gladsome, jubilant, suitable for the expression of lively emotion, such as is common to children, and yet not savour in the slightest degree of slang. In the music of the Sabbath-school, no tunes and no words should be tolerated, the manifest tendency of which is not to produce, not only devout feeling, but a certain refinement and gentleness of feeling. A child may be active, playful, buoyant, brimming over with life, and yet not be rude. We feel instinctively that certain tunes and certain words are rude and unmannerly. They are fit only for clowns. Yet the remedy for this extreme is not to go off into the dreary solemnities of long-metre. It is certainly possible to have our Sabbath-school music buoyant and exhilarating, so as to be a source of the highest gratification to the children, and yet conducive to refinement as well as devotion.

It is a very important thing for the superintendent to be a good singer. It helps him amazingly in conducting a school. There are many times, when a judicious superintendent, if he be a singer himself, can change the whole current of thought and feeling in his school by a little suitable music skilfully thrown in here and there. I have much more faith in singing than in scolding. Yet it is not absolutely essential that the superintendent should be a singer, in order to have good singing in the school. The very best singing in Sabbath-school that I have ever known, was in a school whose superintendent could not sing at all. He had the advantage of a pretty good chorister. But his main reliance, in securing good singing in the school, was in himself. In the first place, he allowed nothing to be sung, the tone of which, both as to words and music, was not perfectly unexceptionable, no matter how great a favourite it might be with the children. So far his action was merely negative. But, in the next place, and as a rule on which he mainly relied for positive results, he allowed nothing to be sung which the children did not take to. If, after the second or third trial, a tune or a hymn seemed to drag, it was inexorably dropped. This was his invariable test, whenever a new piece of music was proposed. Do the children like it? Do they enter into it heartily? Do they seem pleased when it is announced? Is it an evident pleasure and satisfaction to them to sing it? If the answers to these questions were unsatisfactory, no persuasions of the chorister, no arguments to show why it ought to please, no parade of musical authorities in its favour, were of any avail. If, after fair trial, the children themselves did not take to a tune, the tune was *tabu* in that school. The consequence of this course of procedure was, that in time the school was in possession of a large number of tunes, every one of which was a universal favourite with them, and they sang with a heartiness, beauty, and effect, that I have never seen surpassed in a Sabbath-school. Yet the superintendent could not sing at all, and knew nothing of the science of music.

Children without exception are fond of good music. It has become, in the last few years, one of the most powerful means for bringing children into the Sabbath-school. In the mission-schools of our large cities, a great many of the scholars are attracted to the school in the first place by the music.

The teachers literally sing them in. Children, whose parents for some reason do not allow them to enter the school, are often seen hanging with longing ears about the doors and windows, listening to the sweet music, and sometimes even braving punishment rather than forego the pleasure.

Good music is one of the most important means of bringing children into the Sabbath-school, and of keeping them there; while great care should be taken not to employ music in the school which is irreverent, or undevotional, or which has unworthy and degrading associations, care is still more needed on the other hand that it should be of that living and attractive sort which the children love, and in which they can join; any tune or any hymn, which after fair trial it is found the children do not take to, had better be dropped for something which they will take to.

XVIII.

SABBATH-SCHOOL BOOKS AND PAPERS.

No review of Sabbath-school agencies could be counted at all complete, which did not say something of the books and papers which form so much of the stated reading of the scholars. It has indeed come to be regarded as a settled question, that the Sabbath-school, as a matter of course, will have a library, and almost equally a matter of course, that the scholars will be supplied with a weekly or monthly paper. The amount of reading thus furnished to the community is enormous. Few persons have any adequate idea of its extent. These little volumes are despised by many on account of their diminutive size. One big octavo of five hundred or a thousand pages is counted as equal to fifty of these lilliputians, because perchance the big book has as many printer's *ems* as the fifty little books have. But in estimating the amount of reading furnished to the community by any particular class of books, a main item of the account is the number of times each book is likely to be read. In the College library at Princeton, is a collection of books presented to the College thirty years or more ago by the British Government, some two hundred gigantic folios, containing a printed copy of Doomsday Book, and of the other ancient records of the kingdom. Would the historian of the College, in reckoning up the influences by which the minds of its students have been shaped during these last thirty years, dwell much upon the vast amount of reading matter furnished by those stupendous volumes? Probably not one page in the whole collection has been read by a single student in all that time. Certainly there is in that library many a volume, small enough to be carried in the pocket, which in its real influence has singly outweighed the whole of that imperial collection.

No books are read so much as Sabbath-school books, except novels. It is not by any means certain that even novels are an exception. A good, well selected Sabbath-school library, even with the best care and management, is worn out in about three years. Many of the books indeed are lost or destroyed. But most of them are literally worn out by oft-repeated reading. A book taken home by a child is read during the week not only by him, but often by the father and the mother, by brothers and sisters, in fact by a majority of the household. Many a Sabbath-school book is read by not less than one hundred persons during the course of a year. Is this true of any other book, even of the most fashionable novel? What has been said of Sabbath-school books, is true in a still greater degree of

Sabbath-school papers. They are read and re-read, they pass from hand to hand, from family to family, they are often collected from one school, after being used, and sent off to another, and so kept circulating, as long as the paper on which they are printed will hold together.

The big books, the ponderous octavos and quartos of literature, may be compared to the stately oaks and pines left standing in our fields, while these small books of which I am speaking, find their representatives in the innumerable stalks of grass and grain which overspread the entire surface of the ground. We have no accurate record of the actual number of volumes now in the libraries of the Sabbath-schools of the United States. But their number is certainly to be counted by millions, and far exceeds that in all the other public libraries, even counting the libraries in the common schools. When, therefore, we contemplate the number of these books, the number of times each book is read, and also the impressible character of those by whom chiefly they are read, we may well believe them to be a most important agency in the hands of the church for influencing and educating the minds of the young.

Sabbath-school books and papers are read mainly on the Sabbath. They are universally distributed on that day, and are received by the children as legitimate and proper reading for holy time. This defines their character rigorously in one most important particular. No book should find its way into a Sabbath-school library, no paper should be circulated in the Sabbath-school, that is not strictly and distinctly religious in its character. No matter how interesting may be the contents of a book or a paper, no matter how much useful and curious information it may contain, or how poetical and beautiful its sentiments, if it does not distinctly, and with no uncertain sound, inculcate religious and scriptural truth, it has no place or business in the Sabbath-school.

I doubt the propriety of using Sabbath-school books to answer infidel objections. In ninety-nine cases out of a hundred, it is only bringing these objections for the first time to the child's knowledge. Books for the young should teach positively, not negatively; directly and affirmatively, not controversially. The best way to exclude false ideas on religious subjects from the minds of children, is to preoccupy and fill their minds with true ideas. Each church, too, while it will sedulously teach its youth not only the general doctrines common to all Christians, but also its own distinguishing doctrines as a religious sect, yet will not distract their tender minds with the controversies growing out of these distinguishing doctrines, but rather will reserve such teachings for the books intended for those of a maturer age.

Sabbath-school books, of all others, should be *live* books. It is of no sort of use for publishing-boards to issue, or purchasing-committees to buy, dull books. The children will not read them. If any one wants to see what books are really influencing the children of a Sabbath-school, let him look at the book-case where the library is kept. A single glance will suffice. The shining, unsoiled, good-looking volumes, that stand in unbroken columns on the shelves, may as well be consigned at once to the waste-basket. No matter whose imprimatur they may have, or how ornamental their appearance, their value is simply zero. The real work of the library is done by those volumes which are seldom found for two consecutive weeks on the shelf, and which when there have generally a shockingly bad appearance. Commend me to the book that is blackened and worn, and its pages dog-eared and soiled, its covers broken or gone, its leaves loose, its title-page missing, which hardly holds together, and cannot stand alone on the shelf, and which has to be replaced at least once every twelvemonth. Such a book is not necessarily a good book. But it is unquestionably a *live* book. It is a book that will make its mark in the school.

The very best *preliminary* test of a book for the young is to put it into the hands of young children in a family. If half a dozen books are thus placed within reach of such a group, and it is found that some of the volumes are eagerly devoured, and the reading of them competed for, while others are quietly left on the table, almost unread, these latter may be considered as disposed of, so far as the uses of a Sabbath school library are concerned. It does not follow, however, that the other books are all right, because the children like them. That is only one point, though an indispensable one. Another point in a book, equally indispensable, is the character of its teachings, and of this the children are by no means the proper judges.

It is not easy to lay down a formal rule in regard to the use of fiction in Sabbath-school books. Many books are felt to be unsuitable on this score, though we cannot frame a rule which will exclude them, without excluding others to which we feel no objection. It seems necessary in this matter to judge each book, to a considerable extent, by itself. Love affairs certainly should be kept out of these books. We should exclude also scenes that are overwrought and unnatural, and such as are not likely to have happened, and such as give false ideas of life or of duty, and such as merely excite the feelings without leaving any food for the judgment and the conscience.

XIX.

THE SABBATH-SCHOOL LIBRARY.

ONE of the most perplexing subjects to the superintendent is the management of the Library.

In a large school, the books are destroyed or lost with a wastefulness that is frightful, and yet it seems next to impossible, without a degree of harshness that few superintendents will venture on, to enforce such a degree of responsibility in regard to the use of the books as to prevent this shameful abuse.

The return of the books, the selection of others, and their distribution, take up a large part of the time that the school is in session, and unless the business is conducted with more system than it is in most of the schools, it not only consumes a large amount of time, but it produces endless disorder. Some teachers are not satisfied unless they are allowed to go to the library and make the selection of books for their class by actual inspection of them on the shelves. They take umbrage at the superintendent if he interposes any objection to this course. I have seen schools in which two, or three, or even half a dozen teachers at a time would be at the library, rummaging among the books, while their classes in the meantime would be left to run riot in disorder.

If the superintendent is decided in the matter, and will not allow any such irregular proceedings, then there is dissatisfaction among the scholars. Neither they nor their teachers have any sufficient acquaintance with the books, and the mere title of a book in the catalogue gives little clue to its real character.

They are obliged to select from the caltalogue pretty much at a venture, and when the librarian brings around the books selected, they are found in half the cases utterly unsuitable. A child just beginning to read gets some book of antiquities or of didactic theology. A member of the Bible-class gets a book of nursery rhymes. More frequently still, the book selected is out, or lost, and the scholar gets no book at all.

A valuable book, that has cost fifty cents, or a dollar, is taken home by a poor child. It is borrowed by some of the neighbours and not returned. It is mislaid in the general irregularity and disorder that so often prevail in the homes of the poor, and it cannot be found. It is played with by some of the smaller children, and is so soiled and defaced that it is no longer fit to be placed in the library. The child and its parents are too poor to replace the book, and so there is no remedy. Yet if a dozen such cases occur, as they may easily occur, every week, and without remedy, the library soon disappears altogether.

Besides the loss of time, the waste, the interruption, and disorder, attendant upon the use of the library, there are other evils even more serious. Books creep into our libraries that have no business there. I never saw a Sabbath-school library yet in one of our large city schools, which would not have been enriched by having a goodly portion of its contents committed to the flames. Not that the books are bad, in the sense of containing what is in itself objectionable. But some are merely exciting stories, that convey no religious instruction or Scripture truth. Still more are utterly dull and heavy, such as a child can by no possibility be induced to read. Look over the shelves. You know a book of this kind the moment you see it. There it stands, untouched and clean, year after year.

But how can the evil be avoided? Some of these libraries contain many hundred volumes. They must do so in order to have enough to accommodate the children. But how can the superintendent or the teachers sit down to read all the books that are offered to their choice, and make an intelligent selection? It is impossible. The books now published by the various houses engaged in supplying this species of literature, cannot be less than four thousand. No teacher can expect to be acquainted with them all.

Disturbed by a sense of responsibility in this

matter, and vexed by the petty annoyances which the library gives in the school, some superintendents are disposed at times to throw the whole thing overboard, and not to have any library in the school at all. This would certainly be a great mistake. I speak from no small experience in this matter, and from actual observation among the class of people to whom the Sabbath-school itself is most important, and I feel quite sure that the institution would be shorn of one of its main elements of usefulness, if the library were abandoned. The library book, and the child's paper, carry the blessed influence of the Sabbath-school home to the father and the mother, to the older and the younger children, to friends and neighbours. These silent messengers preach weekly to hundreds of thousands who can be reached by no other agency. By means of the library, skilfully used, the teacher may continue and supplement his lessons all the week round. The library, therefore, cannot be given up. It is too great an element of usefulness. It is too dear to the children, particularly to the children of the poor.

Cannot the difficulties of its management be remedied?

The main difficulties, in my opinion, are two, first in getting a proper selection of books; and second, in having the teachers sufficiently acquainted with them. These two points once secured, there is no other difficulty that cannot be readily met by any superintendent of ordinary executive ability. If the library contains no trash, that is, if there is in it no book that is not both valuable and attractive, and if the teachers in the main are so far informed in regard to the books as to guide the children intelligently in their selections, all the other troubles can be managed without difficulty.

It is in large congregational schools chiefly that these difficulties are felt. The pioneer mission-schools of the West and of the interior do not suffer to the same extent. Such schools do not average over thirty scholars. A ten-dollar library of fifty, or a hundred volumes, is ample for their wants. The librarian of such a school, or the superintendent, if there be no separate officer for the library, can manage the matter without difficulty. But in our large city-schools the case is quite different. There the scholars are numbered by hundreds, and the books in the library often are not less than a thousand volumes.

The time was when a teacher might, without much difficulty, be acquainted with all the books in the market suitable for a child's Sabbath reading. But that time is past. There are a few excellent books with which nearly all the teachers are acquainted. Perhaps in the whole catalogue of one of these large libraries there may be fifty books, possibly a hundred, of which something is known, either by the teacher or by some one of the scholars, in every class. These few books are in constant demand.

There will be perhaps a dozen applications the same day for a single book. Consequently eleven out of the twelve who apply for that book are disappointed. Even where each child is allowed to have three or four choices, such is the run on the few books which are really popular and well known, that half the time no one book out of the three or four books called for is to be had. Out of a class of ten children, in a school that has a library of a thousand volumes, four children perhaps will receive for answer that the books for which they applied are out, four will get books so utterly unsuited to them that they do not even take them home, and two possibly will be suited. I assure the reader, this is no fiction. I have myself seen it, week after week, in hundreds of instances.

I have seen fully one half the session of the school occupied by a class in making its selection of library books, and after all no better result obtained than this. The teacher is not, and from the nature of the case cannot be, acquainted with the character of the books, and consequently he can give no help to the scholars in making the selection. It is a mere lottery, with the chances sadly against success, and it gives endless trouble, vexation, and disappointment.

The evil might be remedied to some extent by having a good descriptive catalogue. In such a catalogue not only the name of each book should be given, but such a description of its character and contents as to enable the teachers and scholars to choose with some degree of intelligence. But where is the superintendent, or where are the teachers, that will undertake to read through a thousand or fifteen hundred volumes, and prepare such a statement of their contents? Even were this possible, the expense would have to be considered. Such a catalogue would make of itself quite a volume, the printing of which would cost enough to supply a pretty fair library.

The only effectual remedy that I can see, is to reduce very materially the number of books selected for a library, and to multiply copies of the books thus selected. It might have three, four, five, or even ten copies of each book on the catalogue, according to the size of the school, or the demand for particular books. If the school be of such a size as to require a thousand volumes, instead of having a thousand separate publications, and a single copy of each, it would be far better to take only the very cream of those in the market, and to have a number of copies of each. This plan is now adopted in all the public Circulating Libraries. Whenever a new book is issued, on which there is likely to be a run, the Library buys a large number of copies. In the case of a Sabbath-school library on this plan, with a limited number of publications, but numerous copies of each, the teachers and the superintendents might reasonably be expected to make themselves acquainted with the character of the greater part of the books. A full descriptive catalogue also might be made without too great labour or expense. Every scholar finally would have a reasonable chance of being suited weekly with a book. It would take two or three years for the books to make the entire circuit of the school, by the end of which time the best of them would be worn out, and the others might be given away, and a new library be purchased.

There are some difficulties connected with the management of the Sabbath-school library which require for their removal merely good business habits and abilities on the part of the librarian. But, as before observed, there are two difficulties not reached by ordinary business methods. The first of these is the selection of the right kind of books in furnishing the library. Out of nearly four thousand separate publications now set before the teachers, as candidates for a place in the library, there is of necessity a large amount of trash, and no small amount that is worse than trash. It is to many teachers and superintendents an appalling task, under the circumstances, to undertake to make an intelligent choice. The other difficulty, to which also I have referred, is the need that the children have for guidance in choosing from the books that are in the library. The remedies for this are twofold. First, the catalogue, instead of being, as it usually is, a mere meagre list of titles of books, should be of a descriptive character, full enough at least to give some clue to the character and adaptedness of each volume. Secondly, teachers should make it a point, more than they now do, to become acquainted with the library. If it were possible, every teacher should know the character of every book in the library. To make even an approximation to this possible, the number of books, (not of volumes, but of separate publications,) must be greatly reduced.

XX.

SABBATH-SCHOOLS AND CHRISTIAN MISSIONS.

The term Missions is here used in its common acceptation. I mean by it all those agencies by which the church is seeking to propagate the gospel beyond its own bounds. Missions among the heathen constitute, by general consent, the largest and most important item in this work. But besides the foreign missionary field, there is much to be done in our own land, which every one recognizes as being of the true missionary character. The work, however, is one, whether done among the pagans of China and Japan, or among the practical heathen of Christian lands. It is to make known the blessed gospel of Jesus Christ to the degraded and ignorant of every land. Its scope and warrant are to be found in that last command of the ascending Saviour: "Go ye into all the world and preach the gospel to every creature."

Should the children in our Sabbath-schools be enlisted in this work? Should our Sabbath-schools, as such, use their organization for the promotion of the mission cause? Should the classes and the schools be formed into missionary societies? These are eminently practical questions? The answers given to them affect materially the character of the schools and the support of the mission cause.

It is alleged by some that children have no money of their own to give; that the money contributed nominally by them is really from their parents, who bestow it for that purpose; that the children are thus educated to believe they are generous and liberal in doing that which costs them nothing; and that finally their attention is distracted, and the legitimate purpose of the school—the study of God's word—is interrupted and hindered by the multiplied machinery of societies, and committees, and collections incident upon this mission enterprise.

It is not to be denied that serious mistakes have been committed in the prosecution of the missionary cause in Sabbath-schools. A school may be converted into a mere machine for collecting money. When such is the case, it is a grievous evil, alike to the mission cause and the Sabbath-school cause. But such a result is not a necessary one, nor is it a common one. On the contrary, the cases are, according to my observation, quite exceptional. Those schools which have most of the missionary spirit, and do most for the cause, are usually the best as schools. They are most flourishing as to numbers, they are the best organized, they are making the best progress in scriptural knowledge, and they record annually the greatest number of conversions.

It is not true that children have no money of

their own. Some parents give to their children a stated allowance, with the express understanding that it may be used in any way the children please, unless for something wrong or forbidden. This allowance is intended as part of their education. It is to train them to a knowledge of the right uses of money. It is therefore most important to keep before the minds of such children the noble ends for which money may be used, and to lead them, from their earliest years, to feel that they, like all others, must exercise self-denial in order to do good. Besides what is thus allowed to some children as pocket money, many young persons are in the habit of earning small sums by voluntary services in time which is allowed them as their own by their parents. It is obvious that money thus acquired is a legitimate subject for beneficence. Children in these circumstances are in danger of two evils, the opposite of each other. They are in danger of becoming spendthrifts on the one side, or on the other of becoming misers. It is therefore rendering them a most important service to educate their consciences to the duty of giving, to cultivate their sensibilities by presenting to them the destitute condition of those who are without the gospel, and to induce them voluntarily, as a matter of duty and of compassion, to be economical and thrifty on the one side, in order to their being liberal and charitable on the other.

Besides the money which children give of their

own, they make excellent collectors. Few persons like to refuse an application from a young child for money for the missionary cause. Nor do these small sums, thus bestowed by fathers, and mothers, and aunts, and uncles, and guests, to help fill up the little one's missionary box, diminish aught from the contributions which these persons give in their own name for the same cause. On the contrary, their hearts are rather warmed towards the cause by seeing the interest which it has enlisted in the heart of their darling. Giving begets giving. Giving to please the little one, makes it only a greater pleasure to give on their own account.

Children should be instructed in this matter.

In the first place, the duty of doing good and of self-denial, as taught in the Scriptures, should be carefully taught them. This is a part of that Bible knowledge which it is the object of the Sabbath-school to inculcate. The passages of Scripture which enjoin the duty of giving, or which contain examples of it, should be hunted up and explained, and made familiar. Such a study will be of the utmost advantage to them and to the church. Christian people are, in the main, sadly deficient in precisely this kind of Scripture knowledge.

In the next place, the children should be made acquainted with the work of Christian missions. The school and the classes should be furnished with missionary maps and charts, so that the scholars can become familiar with the principal localities in which missionaries are operating. Missionary narratives should be put into their hands, or be told to them. They should be instructed in regard to the debasing idolatries of the heathen, and the dreadful cruelties practised among idolaters. When any particular church or denomination has become identified with some special field among the heathen, let the children of that church or denomination be instructed in the fact, that they may grow up with the feeling of a sort of personal interest in it.

In the third place, teachers and superintendents should seek to create among the children a missionary spirit. By this is meant, not merely liberality in giving, and zeal in collecting money, but a love for the work itself. This will be indeed a legitimate result of the two previous provisions. If the young are well instructed in what the Scripture teach as to this great matter, and in what the church is doing in carrying it out, they can hardly fail to fall in with the general current of Christian feeling. They will come to regard their missionary society as being so called, not because it collects money for missions, but because its members all have the missionary spirit, and are in fact, in a very important sense, all missionaries. A school that is so organized, and so animated, will not only raise money largely for the support of missions, but its own members will be found from time to time filling the missionary ranks.

There are several reasons why children especially should be enlisted in the missionary cause.

In the first place, the young have a special interest in that gospel which it is the object of missions to propagate. If the human race were divided into two classes, say white men and red men, and a religion had been revealed which contained provisions for one class only, we would not expect the other class to take any interest in the extension of such a religion. They might not oppose it. But it would certainly be futile to expect of them active, hearty co-operation in propagating it. Some persons seem to regard the young as in like manner virtually excluded from active co-operation in the propagation of the gospel. We have not so learned Christ. Not only are children included in the gospel offer, by virtue of their being rational, accountable, and sinful creatures, and sharing in the general qualities of the race, but the Bible has numerous specific promises and commands made to them directly. Our Saviour himself placed this point beyond all question or cavil by his own memorable words and example. Children were never counted intruders in his presence. He approved and encouraged their attempts to do him honour. The fond mothers who elbowed their way through the crowd and thrust their little ones upon his attention were not repelled as being forward and obtrusive. His rebukes, on the contrary, were reserved for those who thought it indecorous to occupy the Saviour's time with mere children. He stopped his discourse to his adult hearers, in order to talk to the children, and to leave on record a most precious lesson for them particularly. Like a fond father, he placed his hand upon their heads and blessed them. Like a fond mother, he took them in his arms and gave them a loving caress. His words to them, his words of them, were those of gentleness, and love, and warmest sympathy, as if recalling his own childhood and the fond endearments which had been grateful to himself when a babe in Mary's arms. There is, in the life of man, no age towards which the Saviour himself has shown a warmer sympathy; no age in regard to which the Bible has given more specific words of counsel, instruction, and promise; there is no age during which, in point of fact, a larger portion of actual conversions into the kingdom do take place, than the season of youth. It was, therefore, no mere figure of speech when the Saviour said, "Theirs is the kingdom of heaven." The young, therefore, have a right to be taken into the firm, as partners, in this great enterprise of propagating the gospel. It is spreading a blessing of which they are partakers. It is extending an estate in which they are inheritors. This is no forced or fanciful view of the matter, as any one can testify who has had experience in cultivating the missionary spirit among children. They enter into the work with the warmest enthusiasm, and very early acquire a lively personal interest in it. They become identified with it, as something which concerns themselves.

In the second place, missionary labour, whether in the foreign field or at home, has to do mainly with the young. Missionaries, of course, do not neglect the adult. But they find it exceedingly hard, up-hill work to convert a pagan who has been thoroughly confirmed in idolatrous practices, or to reform an immoral man who has spent a long life in sin. Hence all our missionaries, everywhere, direct their main energies to the young. The school, even more than the church, is at first the scene of their labours. If the problem be to reclaim here at home some city suburb, or some vile neighbourhood, which has become too bad for successful interposition, even by the police, the first step by Christian people who would bring about a change, is to plant a mission-school and bring in the miserable, outcast children. So, in heathen lands. The missionaries are often hooted at, and scorned, and maltreated by the men and women, who remain a long time insensible to kindness, and unapproachable by argument. But the confidence of the children is soon won. That same benignity which drew the Jewish children towards Jesus, draws the young Chinese and Hindoos to his disciples. Their affection and their confidence are won by kindness. Heathen children, as well as the children of the vicious and degraded in Christian lands, have usually a hard time of it. Their life is one of wretchedness and neglect. The misery of their condition makes them appreciate more keenly the loving and truthful treatment which they receive from the missionaries. It is so unlike that which they receive from their unnatural parents. This fact, then, that missionary work is chiefly done among and for children, is a reason why children should be interested in it, and take a part in it. There is in fact no more ready way of enlisting the hearts of the young in missions, than by describing to them vividly and truthfully the forlorn condition of heathen children. In every Sabbath-school, and in every family, teachers and parents should take pains to supply the children with suitable missionary reading in books and papers, and to instruct them in various ways in regard to the true condition of those born in heathen lands. Addresses from returned missionaries are most useful in this respect. A missionary museum is a good thing. But there is no end to the ways in which the interest of the young can be excited, if only their teachers and parents have their own hearts in the work.

A third reason why Sabbath-schools should be organized into missionary associations, is that when the scholars become men and women, they will be more likely to take through life an active interest in this great cause. In fact, when a whole congregation thus from childhood grows up with the habit of working in the cause, the habit becomes fixed. It becomes taken for granted that every one is to work for this cause, and to contribute to it. It is too obvious to need argument, that a congregation thus trained is more to be relied on for a steady and liberal support of missions, than one in which the whole matter is left to be argued and demonstrated solely among the adults. Any denomination is wise, which by its ecclesiastical arrangements fosters the policy of enlisting all its youth, through its Sabbath-schools, in the work of propagating the gospel. Some of our most influential denominations have already distinctly inaugurated such a policy, and with the most marked and happy effect.

Nor is it a light argument for this course, that it is in the power of the church, by means of its Sabbath-schools, greatly to swell the general volume of benevolence. It is by means of the Sabbath-school mainly that the duty of giving can be brought home to all, instead of being left, as it now too much is left, to a few. A hundred dollars contributed by a Sabbath-school, comes from much more numerous contributors than a like amount coming from a congregation. This in itself is a great gain. It is of great importance to the well-being of any church, that every man, woman, and child, should be in the habit of giving to the cause of Christ. Then, these small contributions gathered up in the Sabbath-school, though individually diminutive, become mighty in the aggregate. There is not a Christian church in the land which could not double the amount of its annual contributions to the missionary cause, by a thoroughly organized system of missionary associations in its Sabbath-schools. A penny a week from all the Sabbath-school children in the United States, would make an annual contribution of two millions of dollars.

God bless the Sabbath-school Missionary Societies!

XXI.

THE SABBATH-SCHOOL SUPERINTENDENT.

The Superintendent needs to be all that the teacher is—*and something more.* If a person were to undertake, therefore, to describe a good superintendent, one way would be, first, to give all the particulars necessary to a good teacher, and then give the additional requirements needed in the superintendent. As it is my purpose to say something hereafter in regard to the qualifications of teachers, in the few remarks now to be made respecting the superintendent, I shall limit myself to those things which he needs besides being a good teacher. I shall assume that he is pious, prayerful, patient, punctual, persevering, and the like. To speak of these things, in describing a superintendent, is no more necessary than it would be, in describing a physician, to say that he must be a man. A person may be very good, and even a good teacher, without being a good superintendent. What, then, are some of the special things to be looked for in this important office?

In the first place, a Sabbath-school superintendent should have those general executive abilities which are needed in the head of any large business, whether it be that of a store, a bank, a farm, a railroad, a factory, a ship, or an army. He must have what in worldly affairs are called business qualities, and he must have a talent for directing the energies of others. Whoever has the talents necessary for a good manager in any large secular business, has the first qualification of a good superintendent. Such a man must have a strong will. He need not be stubborn, he need not be imperious, he will not be harsh or rude; but he must be a man of strong resolution, and decidedly tenacious in regard to his plans and purposes. There must be a little bit of iron in his composition.

Whoever assumes the headship of any business, with many persons working under him, whether young or old, must know how to use his eyes. Some persons seem to have no faculty whatever for seeing things. They go through the world in a sort of dream. If a man has not a decided talent for observation, he has no business at the head of a school. As a man may have a strong will, without being imperious, boisterous, or rude, so it is not necessary that he should stare, or be sly and tricky, or that he should bustle about much, in order to be a good observer. Looking is not always seeing. There is such a thing as knowing how to see, just as much as there is knowing how to draw a straight line, or knowing how to sing a tune correctly. Two persons, standing side by side, at the superintendent's desk, may look over a school that is in disorder. The one will see exactly where the disorder is, what is its cause, and who is making it. He will detect at a glance who lead, who are led, who are acting thoughtlessly, and who through design. The other will be conscious of a hubbub and a noise, but will see nothing. This power or faculty of seeing is with some a natural gift. But it may be cultivated. The possession of it, in a large degree, whether by nature or cultivation, is absolutely essential to a superintendent.

There must be more than this ability to see. Half a man's power of control over others, especially over the young, is in his eyes. Nor, in order to this power of control, is it necessary to look fierce, or to look cross, or to frown or scowl, or to distort in any manner the features. Brow-beating, like other beating, only hardens the rude and terrifies the gentle. But there is a look, which boys and men alike, and even brutes, recognize as something not to be trifled with. It is a look of conscious authority and power, quiet, composed, resolute— saying, in language which men and brutes alike instinctively understand, that the possessor has deliberately canvassed the question of his right, and of his ability to enforce his requirements, and is ready to go to the full extent of that ability, rather than yield the point of right. All this is conveyed by a quiet, resolute look. The power which some men have in their eyes amounts almost to a fascination. The rebellious spirits of a school-room stand spellbound before it. But let no man attempt to put it on, who is not conscious within himself of the real power which it represents. Children are the last persons in the world to be imposed upon by conceit or superciliousness. They have an intuitive sagacity for detecting pretence. Nor is authority the only power that the superintendent carries in his eye. No instrument of the soul speaks its love so powerfully and so directly to the heart as this. By no means can a man who really loves the young, so quickly win their love. If the superintendent's own heart is full of love for his scholars, and this love beams forth from his eyes, if his face lights up with pleasure whenever he meets them, it will call forth a responding smile from them. It will draw out a ready confidence and affection on their part. This is a part of the mother's wonderful influence. It is the first language of unschooled infancy, and thank God, we never quite forget its meaning or outgrow its power.

It is *not* necessary that a superintendent should be a great talker. More superintendents err by talking too much, than by talking too little. I believe a great many men, who would have made very excellent superintendents, have shrunk from the position, or have not been called to it, because of a false notion, on the part of themselves or their friends, that talking, haranguing the school, was the chief business to be done. Of course, there is a great deal of talking to be done in school. But it is to be done chiefly by the teachers. The busy hum of tongues is for the class, in the active intercourse and play of mind between teacher and scholar. The chief function of the superintendent is so to regulate the affairs of the school that there shall be as little interruption as possible to this close, direct intercommunication between each individual teacher and his class, that there shall be as much solid, compact, unbroken time as possible left to the teacher, after dispatching the necessary public business of the school. The superintendent, who by want of foresight in arranging the order of business, or by an undue loquacity, breaks in seriously upon the time due to the teachers, does great harm. There are cases, indeed, especially in mission-schools, and in schools where a majority of the teachers are very deficient, in which the superintendent is really the master teacher. The teachers, so called, keep the classes together, register the attendance, take in and give out books, and so forth, but have no gift for teaching. They occupy the teacher's seat, because there is no one else to do it. They are the best the superintendent can get, and he is most grateful for their assistance, but he feels obliged to supplement their shortcomings by instruction from the desk. There are, too, speakers with special gifts, for whose speeches the ordinary class instruction of almost any school might very profitably be often suspended. But I am not speaking now of such talkers as these, nor of schools that are quite exceptional in their character. I mean ordinary, regularly organized schools, when I say that the chief function of the superintendent is not haranguing from the desk, and that a man may be a very good superintendent who is not a great talker. Of course, the superintendent must address the school from the desk sometimes. But it should always be done with care and forethought, and with studious and deliberate brevity.

A quality much more important than that of ability in public speaking, is the ability to sing. Even this is not indispensable. Superintendents who know not a note of music, have been able, not only to conduct a school successfully in other respects, but even to secure in the school great excellence in its singing. To do this, however, is to work in the face of manifest difficulties. The superintendent who can sing well, has a gift for his office of inestimable value.

XXII.

THE TEACHER—LOVE FOR THE WORK.

In cities, it is not uncommon to see shop-signs made with a sort of fine lattice work, so arranged and painted as to read differently according to the point from which they are viewed. Approach the shop from the east and you read "Hardware." Approach it from the west and you read "Dry Goods." Stand directly opposite, and the same sign gives only the letters, "Caleb Jones."

Shop signs are not the only things which may have a different reading according to the point from which they are viewed. A man, for instance, has been accustomed to have a quiet Sabbath. He occupies his seat morning and afternoon in the sanctuary, and during the remainder of the sacred day he enjoys a season of calm repose, which he divides between reading and contemplation, with (perhaps?) some little allotment for sleep. But teachers are sadly needed for the Sabbath-school, and some importunate superintendent makes a piteous appeal for help. The call is so loud and long continued that conscience at length is disturbed. The man begins to have a dreamy sort of conviction that possibly this world was not intended for his resting-place; that possibly, in a most important sense, he is his brother's keeper; that perhaps this entire quietude of his Sabbath is not the most effectual mode of discharging his share of the great commission to preach the gospel to every creature. So he begins to look the question seriously in the face, whether indeed he ought not to take a class in the Sabbath-school. But the more he thinks of it, the more onerous does the duty appear. The school which he is invited to join has a reputation of being a very disorderly school. The scholars are rude and unmannerly. Some of the teachers do not belong to his circle, and he is not sure that he will not be in danger of compromising himself in many ways. The school, moreover, has two sessions on the Sabbath, besides a Teachers' Meeting during the week. In addition to this, he understands that the teachers are expected to look after their class out of school, visiting them at their homes, and having a general superintendence over their interests. Altogether, his peace is greatly disturbed by the prospect. He is looking down the east end of the street, and the sign reads nothing but "HARDWARE," in big, staring capitals.

How different often is the feeling of the same man when he is once fairly enlisted in the work. The work indeed was not unduly magnified. He finds it in this respect all that it was represented to be. There is much to do. Many an hour of toil must be encountered. The labour of teaching is not in itself soothing to the nerves. He has to give many a denial to the calls of ease. Yet he finds himself happy; happier, by far, than in his former days of Sabbath composure. The reason is obvious. His heart is in the work. He has become interested in these little ones committed to his care. He goes to meet them at the appointed hour, not like a convict under penalty of the lash, not because he feels that he has to go, or incur somebody's censure, but because it is a pleasure and a privilege to go. It would be a real self-denial to him to stay away. He has learned the benign mystery of Christ's kingdom, that love sweetens every kind of toil. Like his Master, he has now meat to eat that the idler and the worldling know not of. He has learned that active beneficence towards others is often the very best way of kindling the fires of his own devotion. He met Jesus in the way, as he went up that dark alley in search of a poor lame boy. The Holy Ghost was poured out on his own heart as he kneeled by the bed of the sick child in yonder garret. His own conscience was pricked as he hunted for passages by which to awaken the conscience of that careless one. How much more liberal he is than formerly in his donations to benevolent objects! How much more readily his hand finds its way to his purse, and how much wider he opens it! In prayer, too, whether in his private devotions, or in the social meeting, how his heart is opened, how his tongue is unloosed! So far from retrograding in the graces of the Spirit, since the quiet of his Sabbaths was disturbed, he never before made such progress. So far from the Sabbath-school being a burden to him, and a grievance, his Sabbaths were never such seasons of high and precious enjoyment. In fact, to recur once more to our figure, he looks at the shop from a different end of the street. He does not forget, indeed, that there is "hardware" within, but the sign, from the point where he now views it, is all radiant with beauty, while he reads, in letters of living light, "Love, Peace, Joy in the Holy Ghost."

Most sincerely do I pity the teacher who goes to his task from no other motive than a sense of duty. Not only is he thereby a great loser himself, but he lacks one essential qualification for the work which he undertakes. Love not only sweetens toil, but makes it efficacious. If the teacher would succeed in his work, he must love it.

XXIII.

THE TEACHER'S PREPARATION FOR HIS CLASS.

Nothing is plainer than that a man cannot teach what he does not know. He must know a thing himself before he can teach it to others. This is so nearly a truism that it seems trifling to insist upon it. Yet one cannot have much to do with the management of Sabbath-schools without being forced to the conclusion that this is not an accepted truth in the practical beliefs of a great many teachers. I feel, therefore, that it will not be entirely beating the air, if I occupy a few paragraphs in urging upon teachers the duty of study.

Those who neglect weekly preparation for the duties of the Sabbath-school may be divided into several kinds. The first kind consists of those who teach very young children, or very ignorant persons, or who have a miscellaneous class of pupils, with no common lesson. The teacher in such circumstances is apt to suppose that any regular plan of study on his part, in order to prepare himself for the lessons of his class, is not only unnecessary, but impracticable. He has perhaps to hear one scholar read a little out of the Spelling-Book, to help another learn a verse of a hymn or of the Bible, to explain to a third, who is just learning to read, the difference between *b* and *d*, and crooked *s* and round *o*; to hear a fourth recite a page in the catechism; to tell a fifth, who has never before even heard of God, something about the creation, or the fall, or the flood; and he thinks that for such a class all he needs is to be present on the Sabbath, and to go through with a certain amount of hearing lessons, scolding, and telling things that everybody knows. It is a woful mistake. Such a class, beyond all others, requires stated, special preparation on the part of the teacher. The more feeble and ignorant the mind of the learner, the more the teacher must study to find out just what knowledge and ideas are capable of being received by the pupil, and of interesting him. The teacher may have a good deal of knowledge, of one kind and another, without having just what is wanted for his class. He should make it his business on the Sabbath to gauge the minds of his scholars, and during the week to select and prepare for use just those items of knowledge which their case requires and admits. Some persons, who have been engaged for several years in this kind of teaching, have accumulated thereby quite a fund of materials, from which they feel as if they could draw without notice to suit almost any and everybody. But even these persons would do well not to give up the habit of specific preparation for each particular occasion. Without this, instruction is apt to lose its freshness, and to degenerate into mere routine. If a man would understand how much study is necessary in the way of special weekly preparation for a class of mere beginners, let him visit one of the schools for the Feeble-Minded, and see how ingenuity is racked to devise the means of awakening and fixing the attention.

Another teacher is favoured with a more advanced class. His scholars have a regular Bible lesson, with a Question Book from which to learn it. But he has been a great reader all his life, he is familiar with the Bible, has studied and read it a great deal, he is fluent in discourse, often addresses the people in the prayer-meeting, and other occasions, and never seems at a loss for thoughts or for words with which to express them. He is tempted, therefore, to rely upon his general knowledge and fluency, instead of preparing himself specifically upon the lesson of the week. He thinks, if his scholars will study the lesson, he can safely draw enough from his fund of general knowledge to make the subject interesting. So he contents himself with asking the questions that are in the book, and branching off here and there in unpremeditated talk upon something incidentally brought up in the course of the lesson. Such instruction is not entirely lost. But it is far from coming up to that measure of usefulness which every teacher should seek. To a studious child there is no stimulus to study so strong, and at the same time so healthful, as the discovery that his teacher is perfectly at home in every minute point of the lesson. The child feels that his own acquisitions or failures will come under the review of one who can measure them with minute and unerring certainty; and the recollection of this fact operates most powerfully and most beneficially upon the mind of the learner. If the scholar's mind is at all given to inquiry, and there are few minds which have not some tendency in this direction, the thirst for knowledge is stimulated by the certainty that it will be gratified. The more complete and exhaustive is the teacher's knowledge of that particular lesson, the more will the child's natural love for knowledge take root and grow under its influence.

No matter how advanced the teacher may be in knowledge, or how extensive his general acquisitions, he should always aim to bring to each lesson something fresh. This will keep his own mind from stagnation, and it will secure for him a kind of influence over his scholars, which is to be gained in no other way. A sort of preparation which might be good enough for a scholar, will be far from sufficient for the teacher. Nor let the teacher limit his study to books and commentaries. Let him imitate the great Teacher, who drew his instructions from the occurrences of every day. The Sabbath-school teacher would do well to make his book-preparation on Sabbath evening. Let him on that evening go through the ordinary routine of exploring the commentaries and books of reference, and hunting up the parallel passages, so as to have the subject fairly in his mind. Having done this, let him then keep the subject in mind during the week, and be ready to add to his book-knowledge illustrations drawn from life. Let him not study any less, but try to think more. If a teacher is really prepared on a Bible-lesson, say on one of the parables, he can go over the whole thing in his mind, from beginning to end, without once referring either to his Question Book or his Bible. He knows just how and where each turn in the thought comes in, what illustrations he has to give to each; he knows how and where each difficulty arises, and how it is to be met; the whole thing before Saturday night stands out in as full relief before his mind as his scholars do before his eyes on Sabbath morning. This is the kind of preparation needed for successful teaching in the Sabbath-school.

Let it not be forgotten that the man most advanced in knowledge needs to make specific preparation for each lesson, in order rightly to instruct even the most humble and ignorant. The teacher loses the greater part of the benefit to himself and of his power over his class, who relies upon his general knowledge, or his previous acquisitions, instead of preparing himself anew for each particular lesson. The mental food which he offers to his class should be like the manna which the Lord gave to the Israelites, every day fresh from his hands.

The Sabbath-school teacher's thorough preparatory study of his weekly lesson is demanded both by his own wants and those of his class; as without such preparation he can rarely, if ever, rise to the proper fitness for teaching, or secure the respect, attention, and profitable instruction of those whom he teaches.

XXIV.

PUNCTUALITY IN TEACHERS.

It seems as if some people come into the world a little behind time, and they never catch up. They are always and everywhere a little late. The habit is a grievous misfortune to any one. In a teacher, it is mischievous in the extreme. It betrays, too, a lack in the character, which it is difficult to describe by its true name without giving offence. If a teacher is not in his seat at the proper time, he thereby throws the care of his class upon some one else. Either some other teacher, or the superintendent, must do what properly belongs to the one absenting himself. But the superintendent and the other teachers have duties of their own to attend to. Is it right for one person thus, without leave or warning, to throw his own responsibilities upon the shoulders of another? Is there uprightness, or honesty, or any proper and conscientious sense of one's responsibility to the class, to the school, to the superintendent, thus to leave the matter at sixes and sevens, just at the most critical moment in the whole session, namely, at the time of opening?

With what face can a teacher who is late himself admonish his pupils for lateness? Is not such a habit a sin? Does not the teacher who takes a class enter into a virtual engagement to be present, and to be present in time? Because the engagement is voluntary, or informal, is it any less binding on the conscience? Is it not rather, like vows to the Lord, of which no human tribunal can take cognizance, for that very reason all the more sacred? In a worldly point of view, what conduces more to the pleasantness and the success of every kind of enterprise, than punctuality on the part of all engaged? What, on the other hand, is more damaging both to character and prospects, than the want of punctuality? With what unfailing exactness does our heavenly Father observe all his engagements even with sinners! How, without the failure of a second, he brings forth the sun, and the stars, and the seasons at their appointed time! Shall we not, in this as in other things, aim to be perfect, as our Father which is in heaven is perfect?

There is, in the minds of Sabbath-school teachers, not only a woful apathy on this subject, but a singular misapprehension as to what constitutes punctuality. Many teachers seem to suppose that they are in time, if they are present just at the moment when the school begins. It is a great mistake. If the school begins at nine, and the teacher enters exactly at nine, *he is late!* He is at least ten or fifteen minutes late. That a teacher should be in his place some considerable time before the opening of school, is a truth so obvious that it seems hardly worth while to argue it. In many of the public schools, where the theory of what is right and needful takes the form of legal enactment, teachers are required to be in their school-rooms half an hour before the time of beginning school. The superintendent is not able, and does not wish, to play the school Director. But surely we all serve a Master who will take cognizance of shortcomings in duty, and who has a right to something more than a half-way, grudging, scanty service.

There is no time, in the session of a large school, when it is so difficult to maintain order, as in the few moments just before the bell gives the signal for school to begin. Pupils will begin to assemble half an hour before the time. They become more and more numerous as the time advances, and for the last few minutes before school-time, the main body of the scholars will be present. Yet many teachers seem to think that they are fully up to time, if they are present at the moment for opening school. Suppose every teacher should take this ground, what would be the state of the school for the fifteen minutes previous to opening? I recollect once visiting a large city-school, about fifteen minutes before the time for its opening. There were at least two hundred scholars present, and not one teacher on the premises. The scene may be easily imagined. It was a perfect bear-garden. It took half the session of that day to correct the disorder engendered in that fifteen minutes of riot.

It is in vain to say that the children should not be allowed to come until the actual time. This is a thing beyond the power of rules to rectify. Many of the children have no actual time-piece at home. Some come from a distance and cannot time their arrival to a minute. The parents of others want them out of the way, and so send them off to school as soon as breakfast or dinner is over. There will be, therefore, more or less straggling in the arrival of the children at school. Some will come too late, and some will come too early. In a school of any size, there will always be a considerable body of children assembled at least fifteen or twenty minutes before the time for opening, and the teachers must be present to take charge of them and keep them in order. It is on the whole rather desirable that the arrival of the scholars should be thus gradual. Were they all to arrive upon the premises at the same moment, it would lead to great confusion. When they come dropping in, one or two at a time, each scholar can be attended to individually, as he arrives, and all the little adjustments of dress, of overcoats, umbrellas, books, and so forth, can be made by the teacher, so that by the time all are in their seats, all will be thoroughly prepared, and ready for the common duties of the class.

I have seen schools, in which the whole burden of this preliminary preparation was thrown upon the superintendent. *He* was expected to be in his place half an hour, or a quarter of an hour, before the time, while all the other teachers seemed to be quite satisfied with themselves if they entered the door as the bell rang. It would be well if such teachers could change places for a while with the superintendent, and find by experience what it is to stand alone and keep two or three hundred wild children at bay.

The ten or fifteen minutes before school are so exceedingly useful to the teacher, that it is difficult to understand how one whose heart is in the work can stay away. There are so many things needed to be done, which can be better done then than at any other time, that it is indeed surprising how slow teachers are to avail themselves of the privilege. Every teacher has things to say to one scholar or to another, which he does not wish the other members of the class to hear. There is no time so favourable as this for having these little, incidental private talks with individual scholars. Then, too, nearly all the troublesome and time-killing business of library-books and papers can be discharged. Then most of the entries of attendance may be made. Then is the time for entering miscellaneous memoranda in the class-book, and for making general inquiries, and establishing a confidential footing with the different members of the class. In short, a teacher who is in his seat fifteen minutes before school, adds that much to his solid teaching-time after school begins, for the things which he does in those fifteen minutes before school would have otherwise to be done in school, and so his time for teaching would be just thus much abridged.

The Sabbath-school teacher's rigid punctuality in his attendance is essential to the good order of the school, and to the formation of the same habit in his scholars; while the want of it is an example of truancy to them, a disturbance of the arrangements of the school, and a vexation of spirit to those who are appointed to rule over it.

XXV.

IRREGULAR ATTENDANCE OF SABBATH-SCHOOL TEACHERS.

The trials of a Sabbath-school superintendent are many and various. Among these there is none more disheartening than that which arises from the irregular attendance of teachers. If there were not in the Sabbath-school some extraordinary and inherent vitality, it would die out in nine cases out of ten for this single cause. No other business with which we are acquainted could survive the incessant shocks to which this is subjected.

Look at a case. Here is a class of eight or ten boys. Their Sabbath lesson comes only once a week. With all the faithfulness and vigilance that the teacher may give, the chances are that the lesson will be but indifferently learned, even if it has not been forgotten entirely. One boy was absent the last Sabbath and depended upon a classmate to tell him where the lesson would be. That classmate was not attending when the lesson was given out, and so two of the class are entirely unprepared. Thus, for one reason and another, no matter how faithful the teacher may be, the actual progress of the class in Scriptural knowledge is subject to continual drawbacks and interruptions. But let the teacher be absent, and these evils are multiplied indefinitely. In the first place, on the given Sabbath when the teacher is absent, the whole lesson is lost to the whole class. Here is one entire week of religious instruction gone. On the following Sabbath, should the teacher be present, the result will be about the same. The scholars will not know whether to learn a new lesson or the old one, and in the doubt will learn none at all. One day's absence of the teacher does in fact cause the loss of two weeks' instruction. Where there is occasional irregularity of the scholar also, the scholar absent one Sabbath and the teacher the next, all instruction comes to an end. A large experience in this matter has led to the conviction that it takes at least three weeks of diligent attendance on the part of a teacher to repair the injury to his class of one day's absence, and that a teacher who is absent from his post on the average as often as once in four weeks cannot possibly be making any headway. The class will not make any substantial advance in Scriptural knowledge. It is like going up a slippery ascent. It takes three or four strides upward to overcome the loss of a single slip or fall. The man who misses his footing every third or fourth step will never reach the summit. Irregularity in lessons is mischievous enough in the week-day school, where the same subject is pursued from day to day. But where the interval from one lesson to another is an entire week, any considerable interruption or irregularity is fatal.

This is only the first and least of the evils of the irregular attendance of teachers. The children to whom the instructions and influences of the Sabbath-school are most important, are those upon whom the school has least hold. The children of well-ordered and godly families will attend the school whether they are particularly interested or not. If such children, moreover, fail to receive adequate instruction in the school, they have a chance of receiving it at home from their parents. But the larger part of the children in our Sabbath-schools belong to families where God is not feared. This is the class of children to whom the Sabbath-school is of the most vital importance. But to benefit them, it must be made attractive. There is no parental authority behind the child to compel his attendance, if he is disinclined to go. Often it is the reverse. The utmost that can be got from many such parents is a reluctant assent to their children's attendance. It needs no argument to show what must be the effect upon such scholars, of the teacher's failing to meet his class. They gradually lose all interest in the lesson and in the school. They get discouraged. They become irregular in their own attendance. They cease to come altogether. Every superintendent knows how impossible it is to retain such scholars when there is any uncertainty about the teacher's being regularly at his post. The zeal of the superintendent and of his fellow-workers may bring in new recruits by the score. Sabbath after Sabbath new scholars may be registered upon the books. Yet at the end of the year the school is no fuller than it was at the beginning. The punctual teachers generally have their classes full. There is no room for the new scholars with them. So the superintendent is obliged to assign the new scholars to the classes where there are vacancies, and from these classes they soon drop out and disappear as scores of others have done before them. The attempt to fill up such classes is simply to pour water into a sieve. It is all lost labour.

Irregular attendance of the teacher is a source of multiplied evils in the school, besides those produced in his own class. Eight or ten scholars left to themselves, without any one to engage their attention or keep them in order, are a source of annoyance to all the classes in the neighbourhood. If they remain together, they talk, laugh, play, make a noise, practise mischievous pranks upon the children all around them, and so distract the attention and interrupt the lessons of half a dozen classes. If the superintendent distributes them, they still constitute a discordant and disturbing element in every class to which any portion of them is assigned. The superintendent is generally obliged to dispose of vacant classes in this way, in order to prevent disquiet. But it puts a heavy drag upon some three or four other classes. Let every teacher, then, who is absent, remember, first, that all benefit to his own class for that week, and almost all for the week to come, is lost; secondly, that his class will receive a positive injury; thirdly, that he puts a heavy weight and hindrance upon at least three or four of his fellow-teachers; fourthly, that he adds grievously to the cares and perplexities of the superintendent; fifthly, that he contributes more directly and efficiently than any other cause to the promotion of disorder and disquiet in the school; and finally, that it will take him at least three Sabbaths of faithful and diligent attendance to repair the evils of one day's absence.

What would be thought of a preacher who should fail to meet his congregation at the appointed hour? —of a physician who should neglect to visit his patient?—of a clerk who did not attend at the appointed hours of business?—of a lawyer who was not in court when his case was called up?—of a servant who should neglect to prepare the family dinner?—of a man or woman in any relation of life, who should fail to meet a stated engagement, and not only make no provision for the contingency, but neglect even to apprise the parties concerned of the failure, until it was too late to make other arrangements? There is not a business in life that would not be utterly disarranged and brought to a stand-still, if the parties engaged in it were to pursue the course adopted without apparent compunction by some teachers of Sabbath-schools. Such a course adopted by an employé in a bank, a counting-house, a day-school, or in any other public or private business, would ensure immediate dismissal from service. It would ruin any man in any of the public professions. It would imply a breach of contract, and entail inevitable loss of character.

Is the obligation of a teacher to meet his class any less binding because it has been voluntarily assumed, and because the labour is not performed for a pecuniary equivalent? Is a service in which one engages for the sake of Christ any less obligatory than one entered upon for a worldly advantage? May a teacher with good conscience be absent from his class for any cause that would not justify him in failing to meet a business engagement? In case of such necessary absence, is he not bound to give timely notice to the superintendent and to procure a substitute, just as a lawyer, a physician, or a minister would do, in a similar case? If at half-past ten on Sabbath morning, when the people were all assembled for public worship, the elders or the sexton were to receive a message that the minister did not feel very well and would not be there that morning, or that he had been called out of town the day before, and they must get somebody else to preach for them, would the congregation be well satisfied with such a course? The unfaithfulness of a teacher to his class may not be as grave an offence as the one supposed. But is it any less truly a sin in the sight of God? Is there any difference in kind, except as there is a difference between a fraud of a thousand dollars and a fraud of a hundred?

I urge these questions with earnestness. No one can visit a large school and see—as he will see—class after class vacant, sometimes half a dozen at once, without feeling that the attention of those who undertake to teach in Sabbath-schools needs to be directed seriously to this point. Every superintendent who reads these remarks knows, from painful experience, that I have not beaten the air.

XXVI.

THE DUTY OF THE TEACHER IN REGARD TO CLASS ORDER.

What the superintendent owes to the school, the teacher owes to his class. The superintendent is responsible for the general order of the school, the teacher for the order of the class. This is so plain that it seems hardly to admit of argument. Yet very many teachers practically ignore this duty altogether. They either cannot keep their classes in order, or they look upon it as something not within the range of their duties. It is not at all uncommon to see a class in Sabbath-school acting in a rude and disorderly manner, in the immediate presence of their teacher, yet with no more recognition of the teacher's presence than if they were out in the open fields, and the teacher sitting composedly by, with no attempt even to interfere, and feeling apparently as if an attempt to interfere on his part would be as much out of place as it would be for him to go up to the superintendent's desk and ring the bell for the purpose of closing school, or of giving out some general order.

Is there not on this subject some great hallucination in the minds of such teachers?

If the disorder in any class becomes so rampant that it can be borne no longer, the superintendent is obliged of course to interfere, not only for the good of that class, but for the good of the school. Or the teacher may find some particular scholar so incorrigible as to oblige him to call in the superior authority of the superintendent. But every such interference, whether voluntarily invoked, or exercised by the superintendent on his own motion, necessarily weakens the authority of the teacher. Every such interference is a censure of the teacher. If the teacher finds himself unable to carry any necessary point of discipline in his class, he must of course get the aid of the superintendent. But let him always remember that this call for help is an admission of weakness, and that none know so well the full force of the admission as his own scholars. Whenever the superintendent is obliged from his desk to admonish any pupil, it is an admonition to the teacher in whose class the pupil is sitting.

So well are these things understood, that when a class is in disorder, unless there is some flagrant outburst requiring to be instantly arrested, a judicious superintendent will aim to check the disorder, in the first place, not by speaking to the class, but by speaking to the teacher. A superintendent, not being occupied specially with any one class, but sending his eye equally over every part of the room, is in a position to know if the discipline is becoming relaxed in any particular quarter; and, as he passes round the room, he can quietly say to one teacher, "Your scholars are reciting more loudly than you are aware;" to another teacher, "I observe that while you are busy registering your library-books, those children at the left end of your class are annoying the scholars on the next bench;" to a third, "When I give out the hymn, or the lesson, I notice that your scholars rarely open their books to find the place;" to a fourth, "Your scholars disturbed the singing a good deal this morning by laughing and playing during that service;" to a fifth, "Your scholars are usually inattentive to the bell, and I have sometimes to wait some time after ringing it, before they come to entire silence;" to a sixth, "When your class is dismissed, I observe that they are quite irregular in their mode of going out, some loitering behind, others rushing down-stairs and making a great noise."

These remarks, however gently and kindly put, are an admonition to the teacher. But they cannot be avoided. If the teacher will not of his own accord notice and correct such things in his class, the superintendent has no choice in the matter. The delinquent must be reminded of his failure in duty. At the same time, such admonitions have a very different effect from that produced by the superintendent's interfering directly to correct the disorder in question. This latter mode paralyzes the arm of the teacher. It says to the class and to the school, that in the opinion of the superintendent the teacher is not able to control his scholars. The other mode, on the contrary, strengthens the teacher, while admonishing him. It says to the scholars, if indeed they happen to hear the remarks at all, that in the opinion of the superintendent, the teacher has in himself all the authority and all the skill needed to maintain order, but he has been a little oblivious.

Every teacher, then, is responsible for the order of his own class. All teachers are not agreed as to what constitutes good order in school. Some are much more exacting than others. But there are a few things to which I suppose there would be no dissenting voice. There should, for instance, be no loud talking, and talking in any class is too loud when it can be distinctly overheard by any other class. A transgression of this rule soon makes a school a babel. Not more than one in a class should speak at the same time. If, when a question is asked, all answer at once, instead of answering in turn as each is called upon, there will of course be great confusion and noise. It is not perhaps possible, in the Sabbath-school, to prevent entirely conversation among the scholars. But the chief talking should be, not between scholars, among themselves, but in a dialogue between scholar and teacher. Again, each scholar should have a particular seat. Without this, there will always be scrambling and pushing, if not worse. No scholar should leave his seat, for any purpose, without the teacher's permission. While one scholar is reciting, or receiving an explanation from the teacher, every other scholar should be required to give attention to it, as much as though it were his own particular exercise.

These things may seem very simple. The general observance of them, however, would work a wonderful change in our schools. But the teacher who will thoroughly enforce these few simple rules, will need to be wide awake. He will have to make himself felt by all the class all the time. Let him remember that reserve is not one of the special qualifications of the teacher. He must learn to *project* himself outward upon his class. He must have the power and the habit of self-assertion. He need not be arrogant and he will not be rude. But he must speak out, and speak as one having authority.

Without order in a class there cannot be much instruction, and it is very doubtful whether the advantage of the little instruction that is given, is not counterbalanced by the mischiefs growing out of the disorder. Disorder in one class is almost sure to breed disorder in others, and there are few schools in which two or three disorderly classes would not seriously damage the whole school.

Disorder not only disturbs the school generally, and is especially unseemly as occurring on the holy

Sabbath, and while engaged in the study of religious truth, but it has a most marked effect upon the mind of the teacher. There are few minds so thoroughly disciplined as not to be more or less thrown out of their balance by this kind of annoyance. While interrupted by these rude noises and trifling behaviour, the teacher loses not only his time, but his patience. His ideas become confused. He forgets what it was he was going to say. All intelligent and thoughtful instruction is at an end.

There is therefore a continual obligation resting on every teacher, to preserve order in his own class; as a matter needful to the quiet of the whole school, and for the best action of his own mind on the lesson during teaching, and especially for the reception of instruction on the part of his scholars; the want of which is demoralizing to the class, destructive to the influence of teaching, and detrimental to the order of the school.

XXVII.

FILLING UP THE TIME.

In some parts of the country, the chief cry of the Sabbath-school is for time. Old-fashioned country congregations, after the morning service, have a sort of nooning, varying in length from half an hour to an hour, during which intervals those living near by go home to their dinner, and those from a distance retire to their wagons, or to the sheds, for a similar purpose, and then come together again for the afternoon sermon, which ends the public services for the day. The only time for the Sabbath-school is in the brief interval between the two sermons. A considerable part even of this little space must be taken up by the superintendent and the librarian, besides what is frittered away by the delay of the congregation in leaving the house. That under these circumstances there should be a scramble for what little time is left, is not surprising. It is rather surprising that any time should be found for the direct business of teaching, and it shows a singular tenacity of life in the Sabbath-school as an institution, that it should survive at all under such circumstances. From all such schools, from superintendent, librarian, and teacher alike, comes the cry for time. No part of the work of the school can be done as it ought to be, because there is not the necessary time for doing it.

There are others, too, in more favourable circumstances, in schools which have a full session of an hour and a half, who seem never to have time enough for all that they have to say to their class. There are teachers who are full of their work, and full of their subject, who never let a moment escape, after the school is opened and the exercises of the class begin, but go straight on through the hour or hour and a half, turning neither to the right hand nor to the left, and whom the bell for closing always finds in the very midst of active, animated work. I have seen many such teachers. Whatever real good is done in the cause, is done mainly by these. There is no difficulty in securing punctual attendance, or preparation of lessons, in the classes of such teachers. Their classes are always full, and generally all are in attendance. The work thrives under their hands. Knowledge among their pupils grows apace.

But such teachers have their counterparts. In the very same school, with the same lesson, it is not uncommon to see teachers who will take their class through the lesson in about ten or fifteen minutes, and then sit for the rest of the hour with not a word to say. The scholars, having no regular occupation, of course become uneasy and restless; they talk and play and make a noise; one discovers that he is thirsty and must go out; another finds that he needs to go across the room to speak to one of the scholars or teachers about something which has just come into his mind; a third recollects something very funny which happened to him on Saturday, and he has to tell it to the scholar sitting next to him; even the teacher having nothing to do, and tired of sitting still, seeks relief from the awkward position by talking to some neighbouring teacher who has been equally expeditious in dispatching the lesson.

This is unfortunately no fancy sketch. Not a superintendent who reads these remarks, but can verify them from his own experience. I do not recollect ever to have visited a school, in which I did not see *some* of these fast teachers,—men and women who could dispatch the longest lesson in fifteen minutes, and then, for the rest of the hour, "have nothing to do." Surely, this is a great evil. There is hardly a greater evil connected with a Sabbath-school. Children had better by far be at home, than be in school unoccupied. Thus congregated, and not suitably employed, they almost inevitably are in mischief. When a teacher assumes the charge of a class, one of the implied engagements into which he enters, is that he will occupy the attention of the class during the whole time of the school, except when their attention is required by the superintendent. If any teacher, whose eyes light upon this paragraph, is conscious of not having come up to the requirements of such a rule, let him seriously consider the matter.

There are various ways by which teachers fill up the time alloted to instruction. Some, after finishing the lesson, let the scholars read out of the Bible, taking verse about, with an occasional word of explanation by the teacher. This is certainly better than sitting still and doing nothing. Any little fragment of time, not otherwise occupied, may thus be used, and sometimes to great advantage. It can never do harm, and it is an effectual stopper to the dreadful evil of doing nothing. Other teachers fill up the time by telling the children stories. If the teacher has a special gift for this, it may do well enough as an occasional thing. But few persons have the faculty of telling Bible stories, or any other stories, well. Besides, when this kind of matter is relied upon as the main staple for filling up time, it begets an unhealthy feeling among the children, and it is a great temptation to the teacher to fall into loose habits concerning truth. Still, there are many worse things in Sabbath-school than telling the children good stories, and I would not entirely discourage the practice, especially among small children. Others, when at a loss for something to do, read to their class out of a book, or out of a religious paper. Even this, though betokening great poverty of invention on the part of the teacher, is better than nothing.

The proper plan, undoubtedly, for filling up time,

is for the teacher to come to his class so furnished with knowledge in regard to the lesson, that the lesson alone will fill up every moment at his disposal. If the teacher will use due diligence during the week in studying the lesson, and in collecting facts and thoughts in regard to it, he can hardly fail to have matter enough to fill up the whole time of even the longest session. Nor is it necessary for the attainment of this end that the teacher should be a person of great learning, or a very superior scholar. Persons of quite moderate abilities, and of very limited education, often make most instructive teachers. But it is because their heart is in the work. Their mind is occupied through the week with the lesson which they are to give to their class on the Sabbath, and they go about gleaning little by little, in their daily walks, picking up it may be but a straw at a time; but by the time the Sabbath comes, their hands are full; they have quite a sheaf.

One thing every teacher should settle in his mind. He is derelict in his duty, if he does not occupy the attention of his class with *something* the whole of the time allotted to him. The very least he can do is to keep them busy. The teacher who cannot, or who will not, do this, should resign.

Every teacher should feel under strong obligations *fully to occupy the time* of every session that is devoted to instruction; employing it, if possible, in the topics of the lesson under examination, or in such ways as will interest fully, and instruct wisely, those committed to his charge—remembering that the waste minutes of Sabbath-school hours are the seeds of time which Satan sows for a speedy harvest of mischief and sin.

XXVIII.

VISITING SCHOLARS.

FEW, even of teachers, appreciate fully the influence of the heart upon the head. How slow the mind is to receive or understand that to which the heart is averse. On the contrary, how readily we take in knowledge which is pleasing. Aversion to a subject, or to the person who presents it, has a sort of blinding influence upon the mental vision. A wise ancient has told us, indeed, that it is right to learn even from an enemy. But it is the very difficulty of so doing which has given to this saying its chief celebrity. Much of the up-hill work in the training of the young has been because the young have regarded, and often with good reason, the race of teachers as their natural foes. This unhappy idea, when it once takes possession of a child, has the effect of placing him in an attitude of resistance against instruction. Whatever knowledge the teacher succeeds in putting into the mind of such a child, is by the hardest labour. The skilful advocate before a jury knows that much of his success in producing conviction depends upon his first creating a pleasant impression on their minds. Those advocates who are most successful always pave the way for their arguments by adroit speeches, intended simply to gain the confidence and good will of the hearers. To the public speaker of any kind, the willing ear is an indispensable element of success.

Religious teaching, beyond every other kind of teaching, depends for its success upon the good will and affection of the pupil. There are many reasons for this. In the first place, attendance upon religious instruction is voluntary to a much greater extent than attendance upon other studies. Then, it is one of the direct effects of sin to make the mind averse to religious knowledge. Sin moreover has vitiated the taste and corrupted the judgments, so that there are no topics on which even children have so much to unlearn, as they do on those connected with religion. The subject, therefore, more than most subjects, needs to be made attractive. Now nothing so gilds any theme, as love for the one who propounds it. Love is indeed a great beautifier. It makes the plainest pictures comely, the dullest subject entertaining. The teacher who has the love of his scholars, may lead them through almost any path, however hard or strait. Wherever he goes, they will follow.

The connection of these remarks with the subject proposed, is sufficiently obvious. There is no more certain way of gaining the confidence and affections of a Sabbath-school scholar, than by visiting him at his own home. The scholar is pleased with such a visit as a mere attention from one who is his senior and superior. It shows by a significant fact that the scholar is really on his teacher's mind. Such a visit gives an opportunity for getting acquainted with the child, and finding out his peculiarities, and also for learning better his advantages and disadvantages. It brings about also a better understanding between the teacher and the parents, thereby securing active home co-operation. When a teacher thus pays an occasional kindly visit to the members of his class, the scholars and the parents come to regard him as a personal friend. In the case of poor families particularly, these visits are greatly prized. Such families often make the teacher a sort of general counsellor and adviser, even in worldly affairs. The kind and pleasant relations thus established between the teacher and the homes of his scholars, give him a wonderfully increased power over them in the class. Instruction and advice from his lips are quite a different thing from what the same words would be coming from a stranger. Besides, the teacher who knows all the circumstances of the child's home, knows better how to adapt his instructions to each particular case. He himself too becomes more interested in each. His own sympathies are awakened, as well as those of his scholars. The work of the class, from being a drudgery and a dull routine, becomes a living, animating process. He teaches with half the toil, because with twice the interest, that he formerly taught.

Not the least among the benefits of this visitation of scholars, is that it breaks up almost entirely that irregularity of attendance, which is the greatest weakness of the Sabbath-school system. If it gets to be understood that a teacher will visit all his scholars regularly at certain intervals, and that he will invariably visit in the case of every absence, absenteeism, except for satisfactory causes, will soon cease. A scholar, whose absence is thus immediately followed up by a visit from the teacher, will either be shamed out of it, if the absence were unnecessary, and he will cease to be delinquent, or else he will leave school entirely, which is certainly a better result than the fitful, irregular, profitless attendance given by many scholars. A school with one hundred scholars, all of whom attend regularly, does more good by far than a school of one hundred and fifty scholars, which maintains an average attendance of only one hundred. Visiting has an effect upon the preparation of lessons almost equal to that upon the attendance. It gives the teacher a chance of seeing exactly what opportunities for study the children have, and of explaining to the parents exactly what kind of preparation is needed. There are few parents who are not pleased with this kindly interest in their own children, and who will not gladly co-operate with the teacher in securing the beneficent ends for which he is labouring. The reason that many parents do so little of this much needed co-operation is that they really do not know how. A little pleasant intercourse with the teacher sets the whole thing right. The teacher, if a judicious person, can do in this way an important service to parents, giving them most valuable hints and suggestions in regard to the religious training of their children.

It is not necessary that the visits of a Sabbath-school teacher to his scholars at their homes should be always what is called a religious visit. Of course it should not be characterized by anything frivolous. But it is not necessary, at such a visit, always to introduce the subject of religion. Many young teachers are deterred from discharging this duty by an incorrect impression on this point. The visit being on a week-day, any subject of conversation will be proper, which is proper between two Christians meeting on a week-day. The primary object of the visit is not to impart religious instruction, but to establish and strengthen kind and friendly relations, to acquire information in regard to the domestic influences which surround the child, and to gain his confidence. At the same time, if the teacher is drawn to open his mouth to a scholar on the subject of personal religion, he will often find precious opportunities in the course of these visits.

The question, how often a teacher should visit the members of his class, does not admit of any absolute rule. There are some points in regard to it, however, which every teacher ought to regard as fixed. First, the general duty should be admitted. Each scholar should be visited statedly by his teacher. Whether the teacher should visit his scholars once a week, once a month, once a year, or once in any given time, are questions of degree. The first postulate is the duty of visiting at all. To that demand there should be no denial. From a pretty extended experience and observation in regard to the question of frequency, I am inclined to think that the stated visitations of the class ought to range between one month and three months. Classes require more or less visitation according to circumstances and age. The teacher is not in danger of erring on the side of frequency. Another point of vital importance, even more important than the first, is the duty of visiting immediately every absentee. This visit should be made if possible on the very day, before the Sabbath is over, and should never be postponed longer than Monday or Tuesday, if it can be avoided. If the child is sick, the visit will be most welcome, and all the more so for being prompt. If the absence is through indifference or neglect, the promptness of the teacher's call will be more efficient as a reproof and correction than any amount of words could be. If it once gets to be known that in case of absence the teacher will invariably call before the next Sabbath, there will be very few such calls to be made. The teacher's class will be always full.

The success of every teacher will depend much on his frequent friendly and Christian visitation of his scholars; thus availing himself of the sympathy of parents and children, begetting a reciprocal kindness, exciting his own interest in duty, and preparing the soil of the heart for the proper culture of Sabbath-school instruction.

XXIX.

THE TEACHER'S DAILY WALK.

EXAMPLE is the most powerful of all teachers. This is true in regard to every kind of knowledge. Even in mechanical employments, we learn how to do a thing sooner by seeing others do it than by hearing explanations of the process. Verbal explanations are necessary, and they have their place. But with these alone, the apprentice would find it slow work learning a trade. How long would it take a boy to learn to handle an axe, or a saw, or a plough, or a graver's tool, to learn moulding, type-founding, or type-setting, by hearing lectures on these arts? The talking may be very well, and perhaps in learning some of the trades, the master mechanic does not give to the apprentice enough of this verbal explanation. But the indispensable part after all, in a boy's learning a trade, is his *seeing* the work done. It is by imitation mainly that we become adepts.

So in imparting intellectual knowledge, the principle of imitation has its place. A child learns arithmetic, not merely by hearing of the relations of numbers, but by seeing others go through the various arithmetical processes. He learns how to study, not merely by being exhorted to it as a duty, but by seeing others study.

Example is something more even than a means of teaching. It is contagious. We not only learn how to do a thing by seeing it done, but the sight of it in others is persuasive to us to do it ourselves. Example allures as well as teaches. It leads to imitation in evil as well as good. One crime is often the parent of others. So well is this understood, that legislators in many parts of the world have now ordered all executions for crime to be made in private. The terror of punishment as a motive to deter others from crime, is not so powerful as is the example itself in producing imitations. Criminal statistics abundantly prove that public hangings for murder have been among the most prolific provocatives of murder. Such works as "The Pirate's Own Book," no matter how truthful may be their records, or how faithfully they may portray the dreadful end of crime, are yet most fruitful sources of crime. It is as if the reader saw the wicked deed; and it is a well understood principle of human nature, that what we see done we are instinctively tempted to do ourselves.

The power of example is felt in no subject more than in religion, and no religious persons, as a class, are more looked to than Sabbath-school teachers. They are, whether rightly or wrongly, considered as being more decidedly religious than ordinary members of the church. The young especially look to them as examples. The power of this feeling in a child's mind is very great. No presentation of truth in maturer years ever brings it with such power upon the heart and conscience, as this living example of the teacher of his childhood. So also nothing sooner shakes the faith of childhood than any dereliction of duty on the part of a religious teacher. I knew some years since a most painful instance of this. The teacher of a class of boys in Sabbath-school, was detected in a gross crime and had to flee from the country. He had been very active in his religious duties, and his scholars were completely wrapped up in him. They thought him almost perfection. He was to them a living gospel. The father of one of the boys, having heard of the crime, and fearing the effect the knowledge of it might produce upon his child, took pains to break the discovery to him gradually and cautiously. The little fellow was on the floor at the time, amusing himself with some childish game. When the announcement was made, the moment the real truth flashed upon his mind, he started as if struck with sudden pain, his playthings dropped instantly from his hands, a cry of distress rose from his lips, he turned pale as if about to faint. It was weeks and months before his moral nature recovered from the shock. The whole church with which this teacher was connected, was in mourning over his fall. But I doubt whether any one, outside of his own family, felt it so deeply as this young, wounded heart.

The example cited is an extreme case. Yet more young hearts are wounded by the unchristian conduct of their teachers than many suppose. Childhood is confiding. It takes its teachers upon trust. It believes all they say, and looks with reverence upon all they do, until taught otherwise by bitter experience. Not merely on the Sabbath, and in the class, but during the week, and in all his daily business and intercourse, the teacher is observed by his pupils. When they do not see him, they hear of him from others. Whatever is said of him, their greedy ears drink in. His dress, his gait, his manners, his style of living, his style of conversation, his choice of company, whatever he says or does, or leaves undone, in the presence of others, throughout the entire week, constitute a part of his course of instruction to his class. They may not know it all, as indeed they do not hear all he tells them with his own mouth on the Sabbath. But much of it they do know. There is a common fame, that goes out in regard to every man, and none so soon and so surely gather it up, as a man's scholars, and whatever they thus know about a man is a part of his lesson to them. It may perhaps be thought a hard condition of the office of teacher, but it cannot be helped. It is a part of the constitution of things, as much as the law of gravitation. This indirect, unconscious tuition is going on all the while.

It follows from these considerations, that of all men the teacher needs to be circumspect and watchful. It will be in vain for him to urge upon his children on the Sabbath the duty of a religious life, and then spend the remaining days of the week as a worldling. Whatever duty, whatever standard of piety, he sets before them, in his regular lessons, he must exemplify in his own daily walk and conversation. Just so far as he fails, as a living exemplar and pattern of what he teaches, does he make those teachings nugatory. Just so far as he lives up to them, in his daily walks and business, does he give them emphasis and force.

The Sabbath-school teacher's example in all the walks of life, is an influence for good or evil which should admonish him to continual well-doing, that his light may so shine before men, that they seeing his good works may glorify our Father which is in heaven.

XXX.

THE AIM OF THE SABBATH-SCHOOL TEACHER.

When Robert Raikes opened his Sabbath-school in Gloucester, his aim was benevolent and good, but it was not that to which teachers mainly look now. His primary and main intention was to gather vicious and ignorant children out of the street, and to keep them out of harm's way, at least, while teaching them the rudiments of knowledge. They were taught to read and spell, to write and cipher, in connection with good moral and religious instruction. They were taught precisely what other children of the same age were taught in the week-day school, on the other days of the week. His schools were reformatory schools, like those in our present Houses of Refuge. The teachers were paid, and the studies were mainly of a secular kind. It was a scheme of benevolence, the worthy thought of a noble and pious mind. But the primary intention was not that which fills the mind and guides the energies of the Sabbath-school teacher of the present day.

In this country, with rare exceptions, the Sabbath-school is not needed for teaching reading, or for teaching any of the branches of mere secular knowledge. All the branches of a good English education are provided for at the public expense, in the common schools, and may there be learned to better advantage than in the Sabbath-school. There may be particular neighbonrhoods where this is not the case, and there may be in every neighbourhood particular individuals, who, for special reasons, cannot have the benefit of the common week-day school. In such cases, rather than that a child should grow up unable to read God's word, the Sabbath-school teacher would think it no desecration of the holy day to teach a child or a man to read.

But these cases are the exceptions. For all the purposes of a general statement, it is undoubtedly true, that the Sabbath-school is now needed only for religious instruction. The aim of the teacher is restricted to this. Not only so, he aims distinctly, avowedly, directly, at the *conversion* of his scholars. The children of a neighbourhood are improved by the Sabbath-school in their worldly circumstances. A mission-school planted in a degraded and wretched locality, and maintained there for a few years, always works a marked change in the neighbourhood. The people become more orderly, more cleanly, more thrifty; crime diminishes, property rises in value. But these are only the incidents of the teacher's work. He does not establish the school for these ends as his first and main intention. He goes to that wretched neighbourhood to rescue the people from a still more dreadful abode in the world to come. His object is to christianize them. But a man cannot become a Christian without becoming a better citizen. Christianity carries civilization and human progress in its train. In proportion as the teacher limits himself strictly to a religious and christianizing work, will its worldly benefits multiply and abound. If he has a class of ten children, in a mission-school, and he could have the assurance that through his efforts every one of them had become converted and was a true Christian, he would be more certain of having secured a great worldly good to the neighbourhood and to the families in which those children lived, than if he had addressed himself directly to the business of social economy and reform.

The teacher's labours, however, are not inspired by the view of these incidental worldly advantages resulting from them. His soul is stirred within him because the souls of these children are going down to eternal death. He wishes to save them from ruin in the world to come. The child of the rich equally with the child of the poor is exposed to this ruin. The motive, therefore, presses upon every teacher. Teachers in the church-school, no less than teachers in the mission-school, have the burden of souls laid upon them. The first and main inquiry of every teacher, on taking a child into his Sabbath-school class, should be, how shall I compass the conversion and everlasting salvation of this child?

I do not say that the teacher should do nothing else but harangue and exhort his scholars on the subject of personal religion. There must be discretion on this as on other subjects,—perhaps we should say, on this more than on any other subject. There is a mode of urging children to become Christians that is repulsive and hardening. But on the other hand, there is another and a worse extreme, that of never approaching the subject. Some persons teach in Sabbath-schools as if their only object was to amuse the children, or to give them curious and entertaining biblical knowledge. The habit is entirely too rare of making direct, personal appeals to scholars on the subject of their salvation. I fear that teachers are greatly remiss in this very thing. They do not press home the inquiry, as they should, pointedly, tenderly, perseveringly, to each scholar, Are you a Christian? Do you mean to become one? Are you striving to become one? Are you prepared to die?

If this thing is done as a matter of form, or with any show of self-consequence, or obtrusively and indelicately, it will of course be pernicious. But when the question comes as if the teacher could not restrain it, as if his heart was burdened with it, it can hardly fail of a good effect. I do not say that the teacher should press this question directly every Sabbath. But it is my conviction, that he should let no Sabbath pass without making his scholars feel, and if possible *every* scholar feel, that the salvation of their souls is that which brings him to the Sabbath-school. If this great errand is truly in the teacher's heart, the scholar will read it in the tone of his voice, the look of his eye, the quiver of his lip, in his whole carriage and demeanor. If this great errand is truly the very burden of the teacher's soul, he will frequently give it opportune, direct expression. Out of the abundance of the heart the mouth *must* speak.

The great aim of the Sabbath-school teacher should be to bring children to the saving knowledge of Christ. He should not merely recognize this aim in the general, but should keep it constantly before him. He should let no Sabbath pass, as the pastor should let no sermon pass, without making those under his care feel that he is aiming at their conversion.

Teachers will be faithful to every other duty of their position, who are recreant to this. There are teachers whom no stress of business or of weather, and only serious illness, ever keeps from their posts. The lesson is always thoroughly prepared. There is no lack of diligence in hunting up books of reference, tables, maps, charts, pictures, and curiosities of various kinds, in order to make the lesson easy and interesting. Absentees are faithfully and promptly visited. The teacher spends much time in making himself familiar with the books in the library, so as to secure for his scholars a judicious selection of books. The class seems always full and always orderly. The scholars are attentive, and are steadily growing in Scriptural knowledge. There is no class in the room on which the eye of the superintendent rests with greater satisfaction. The teacher is apparently a model teacher. Yet from the beginning of the year to the end, he never urges upon his scholars, either individually or collectively, either in the class or out of the class, the direct question, Are you seeking to become a Christian?

Far be it from me to say that such a teacher does no good. In my own experience and observation I have had too many evidences to the contrary. Labours like these not only do immense good of a general kind, but they often lead ultimately to the conversion of scholars. Persons of adult years often connect themselves with the church by public profession, whose conversion either dates back to the times of their Sabbath-school lessons, or has grown out of the seed quietly and patiently sown in those former years. All this, however, does not change the fact, that had the teacher kindly but courageously pointed his instructions directly home to the consciences of his scholars, had he pressed the question frequently and plainly, What is each one of you doing in the matter of your own personal salvation? the number of conversions would have been greatly increased.

An example of this kind of fidelity fell under my own observation early in life. About forty years ago, two ladies, Philadelphians, went to Wilkesbarre, Pennsylvania, to spend the summer. Having some leisure on their hands, and having their hearts full of their Master's work, they, with another lady, a resident of Wilkesbarre, still living, established a Sabbath-school in an uncultivated neighbourhood, not far from the village. Miss Gardiner, one of the city teachers referred to, was a lady of more than common culture and refinement, and one in whose heart zeal for Christ's cause seemed an ever-burning flame. The class assigned to her was a company of country boys, not very inviting in any respect. This was before the days of "Question Books." The lessons consisted mainly in committing to memory portions of the Scriptures. The portions thus recited were explained, and various devices were resorted to, for the purpose of making the exercises attractive and interesting. But one feature of the service was never wanting. No Sabbath ever passed without the question coming home to the class, "Boys, are you Christians? Do you mean to become Christians? Are you doing any thing to this end? Can you ever do it better than now?" I speak the testimony at least of one of those boys. Not one Sabbath did he ever go home from that school without his conscience being pricked on the duty of giving instant, personal attention to the great business of making his peace with God. Not one Sabbath ever passed on which that faithful teacher failed to seek, by most direct means, *his* conversion. Though the school was held in a barn, and its appointments were all of the rudest kind, it became a heaven on earth to that boy. If he was ever converted at all; if he has ever done any service to the Sabbath-school cause, or to any department of his Master's work, he is most happy, even at this late day, thus publicly, thankfully to trace it to the fidelity of that Christian woman. MARY R. GARDINER, long since gone to her reward. But her memory is still fragrant in at least one grateful heart.

XXXI.

THE INFLUENCE OF THE SABBATH-SCHOOL WORK ON THE TEACHER.

The church is a kind of Normal School. Christ is here training his disciples for that better and higher service expected of them in the world to come. One of the essential conditions of a Normal school is, that there should be connected with it a school of practice, where those in the Normal school, while receiving lessons in the theory of their art, may go in and try their hand by actual experiment. So is it in the church. The Master there teaches to his disciples the lessons of the kingdom. They there learn the theory of the heavenly graces. But he has also his School of Practice, in which they become rapidly proficient in his lessons, and that is by the religious training and instruction of the little ones. If such a thing could be supposed, as that the Sabbath-school was of no benefit whatever to the children, yet such are the extent and variety of the reflex blessings which it brings upon the teachers, that it would still be worth all the labour and money it costs.

Think, in the first place, how rapidly Sabbath-school teachers improve in Scriptural knowledge. All Christians are supposed to study the Scriptures, and to be growing in knowledge. It is undoubtedly the duty of all Christians thus to add continually to their knowledge of divine truth. But human nature is frail at its best estate. We may read the Bible, and read it statedly and attentively. But that is quite a different thing from studying it. It is rarely indeed that people study the Bible, or study anything, unless for some specific purpose. The teacher, who has a class in the Sabbath-school dependent on him for instruction, has just such a motive, statedly recurring. He has every week to make himself master of some particular portion of Scriptural truth. He must not only acquire it, but must make his knowledge of it so definite and precise, that he may communicate it intelligently to others. Hence no class of Christians give to the Bible so much real study, none study it so statedly and systematically, none grow so continually and healthily in Bible knowledge, as Sabbath-school teachers.

Besides this, there is something in the very act of teaching that gives force to the argument. It is a noticeable peculiarity of the human mind, that a man's knowledge is made more certain and definite to himself by the act of communicating it to another. A man, indeed, can hardly be said to know a thing himself until he has told it to somebody else, or has in some way, by tongue or pen, given expression to it. Teaching, we learn. By communicating to others what we have learned of holy Scripture, we clinch the knowledge in our own mind. By imparting it, we only make it the more inalienably our own. Hence the true teacher is always a learner. There is probably no part of a pastor's charge, of which he feels so sure that they are advancing in knowledge, as his corps of faithful Sabbath-school teachers.

If service in the Sabbath-school tends to promote the knowledge of the teacher, much more does it improve his piety. He will have the courage to address a youth on the subject of personal religion, when he would shrink from doing the same to a man or woman. He will pray with a young person, when he would not with one older. By visiting his scholars, he learns how to visit others for religious purposes. His timidity in religious duty gradually wears off. His tongue is unloosed, and he learns the secret of speaking a word in season for his Master. In the social prayer-meeting, and in nearly all religious services, the pastor finds no co-operation equally reliable with that which comes from his band of Sabbath-school teachers. Their every function as teachers is, in fact, some act or emotion of Christian charity; and this queen of the virtues, like all other affections, good or bad, grows by exercise.

Not only does service in the Sabbath-school improve the Scriptural knowledge, and increase the piety of those who are truly pious, but it leads often to the conversion of those who engage in it while unconverted. Thousands upon thousands of unconverted teachers are annually brought into the kingdom. The serious character of the truths which they have to deal with in the lessons of the class, gradually affects their own minds. They are led almost inevitably to reflect upon the importance of being able to speak on these topics from their own experience. They can hardly help thinking how sad it would be if the children of their charge should be saved, while they themselves become "castaway." Often, under the teaching of a sober-minded but unconverted person, children are awakened, and begin to inquire of their teacher, with tears in their eyes, what must they do to be saved. Such inquiries, from these young and tender minds, send conviction to the conscience of the teacher, and lead him to bring home the question to his own soul. I once knew a large school, in which, at its opening, a sufficient number of teachers who were members of the church could not be obtained. During the first year, some eighteen or twenty of the teachers were unconverted persons. Before the end of two years, every one of these teachers was converted and brought into the church. I have never been connected with any Sabbath-school, for any length of time, in which *some* persons were not converted while engaged in teaching. While watering others, they have themselves been watered.

It is indeed the uniform testimony of Christian

pastors and of others having the oversight of souls, that active service in the work of the Sabbath-school is one of the most direct and efficient means of promoting the personal piety of the teacher himself.

XXXII.

THE EMPLOYMENT OF PERSONS IN SABBATH-SCHOOLS WHO ARE NOT PROFESSORS OF RELIGION.

There are not a few, and among them persons of very eminent authority, who object under all circumstances to the employment of any one as a teacher in the Sabbath-school who is not a professing Christian. They contend that there is the same sort of impropriety in an unconverted man's teaching in the Sabbath-school that there would be in his preaching in the church. Teaching, they say, is only another kind of preaching. Teachers and preachers are both ministers of the word, both dispense the same gospel, both dispense it on the same holy day, both have the care of souls, both bring sinners to Christ, both are brought into contact with awakened sinners, and are called upon to give spiritual counsel. Both, therefore, need to know, by their own personal experience, the power and life of those doctrines which they undertake to expound.

In regard to this matter, it should be borne in mind that no one claims that it is desirable to employ unconverted Sabbath-school teachers, where others equally capable can be found, who are professing Christians. Two teachers being proposed, equal in other respects, but one a professor of religion, the other not a professor, no superintendent or pastor would hesitate for a moment as to the choice. Where godly teachers can be found, having even the most moderate qualifications for the office, no superintendent, we believe, ever seeks to bring in teachers who are not members of the church. The superintendent would rather even have the quality of the instruction very much lowered, than run the risk of having it perverted by its being administered by unconverted persons. The only case in which, so far as I know, the employment of such persons is encouraged, is when an adequate supply of church members, suitable for the purpose, cannot be obtained. In such cases, it does seem no light responsibility for a superintendent or a pastor, or whoever has the power in the matter, to refuse the proffered help of a serious-minded, judicious, and educated person, because he is not a professing Christian, and to say to a class of ignorant children, who are willing and ready to receive instruction, You shall not be instructed.

The case is by no means an imaginary one, in either of its parts. There are, in almost every congregation, persons religiously educated, regular attendants upon the sanctuary, upright in their lives, sedate and discreet, who respect religion and mean to become Christians, who perhaps are actually seeking the way of life, and who willingly respond to an invitation of the superintendent for help. Shall the superintendent refuse all such proffered help, even though he is almost in despair for the lack of assistance? Shall he sternly discourage the efforts of such persons to make themselves useful among the young? There are in almost every congregation, particularly in congregations engaged in mission-school work, more scholars to be taught than teachers to take care of them. It is not a rare thing for a superintendent to have to disband a class, or, which amounts to the same thing, allow them gradually to be scattered, through the want of adequate care and instruction. Shall the superintendent let these ignorant wanderers go away unfed and unnurtured, because the only man who can be found to reach to them the bread of life has never tasted it himself?

Is it true that none but a converted man can be the means of good to others? Is it not among the possibilities, is it not even among the recorded and authenticated facts, that an unconverted man may be the means of conversion to others? Does it vitiate the power of a medicine, that it is administered by one who does not take it himself? Is not every man, whether he be converted or not, bound to speak well of Christ, and to recommend his gospel to others? Is there any meaning or obligation in that solemn behest, almost the very last utterance of holy writ, "Let him that *heareth* say, Come?" According to this precious Scripture, not only the Spirit and the Bride, that is, the Church,—professing Christians—proclaim the gospel offer, and invite thirsty souls to come to the water of life, but all men who hear of this joyful news are solemnly exhorted to spread it. "Let EVERY ONE THAT HEARETH say, Come!"

The analogy between the Sabbath-school teacher and the minister is pushed too far. They are indeed alike in very many things. So are all Christians. Every Christian man is bound to promote Christ's kingdom, and so far as he is a Christian at all, he is labouring to bring about this great end, the universal reign of Christ. There is no greater obligation on the minister to seek the glory of Christ and the conversion of men, than there is on every member of his flock. The difference of their obligations are of kind, not of degree. The work of the Sabbath-school teacher is indeed in many things nearer in kind to that of the minister, than is the work of other Christians. Yet it is very far from being the same. Sabbath-school teachers are rather the Levites of our latter dispensation. They do a great deal of useful and necessary work about the tabernacle, but they are not Aaron and Moses, and they do not require solemn, priestly ordination.

It is a fact of continual occurrence, that persons are converted while engaged in the work of Sabbath-school teaching. While so engaged, they are necessarily brought into close quarters with gospel truth. They no longer attend to religion in that sort of passive way which characterizes most church-goers. They are obliged to become active in their habits of attention to divine things. While communicating Scripture knowledge to others, their own conscience is very apt to be pricked. They are, moreover, brought into habits of intimacy with some of the most godly persons in the congregation. Besides this, there is something contagious in the eager response which childhood so often gives to the claims of religion; and a man while sitting before a class of bright eyes and warm hearts, sometimes finds his own soul opening before he is aware of it, to the genial influences of the gospel which he is teaching. It is therefore not to be wondered at that so many persons are brought into the kingdom from the corps of Sabbath-school teachers. It would be a most strange thing if such were not the case.

While advocating, however, for many reasons, the employment of unconverted persons in the work of Sabbath-school teaching, when other teachers of suitable character cannot be obtained, I think there is need of much caution in the matter. In the first place, the superintendent and the pastor should canvass the subject thoroughly, and see if there are not, in the church, members enough living at ease, doing nothing in the way of personal service, whose conscience ought to be stirred up. There are in our churches vast numbers of unemployed members. Let these first be looked after, for their own sake, as well as for the sake of the work. In the next place, the utmost care should be taken not to place frivolous persons, whether members of the church or not, in the responsible and serious position of Sabbath-school teachers. We do not wish to see teachers glum and sour of aspect, whether in the Sabbath-school or the week-day school. Give us, by all means, the teacher with a bright, sunny face, who knows how to smile and look pleased. Joy and gladness are quite consistent with thorough earnestness. But I have been often pained in going into schools, to see teachers whom no stretch of courtesy would enable one to count otherwise than frivolous. Their whole demeanour, dress, conversation, and looks indicate levity. No such person should be allowed to teach in a Sabbath-school.

While, therefore, it is eminently desirable to have teachers who are professing Christians and members of the church, yet where such cannot be obtained in sufficient numbers, and there are persons of good moral character, and religiously inclined, who are willing to engage in the service, they should be encouraged to do so, as there are very numerous examples of such persons being themselves converted while so engaged, and of becoming afterwards most active and useful Christians.

XXXIII.

QUESTION BOOKS AND COMMENTARIES.

No one doubts their value. They are "helps" which teachers are glad to use. When we assemble in Teachers' Meetings, and attempt to prepare ourselves for explaining the lesson to our classes, we all want to hear what the Commentators say, and then we turn and twist the "questions" laid down in the book till we have a precise answer to each. In this way, we often study the Commentary and the Question Book more than the Scripture itself. We get into the habit, too, of thinking that nothing in the Bible is interesting, or worth talking about to our classes, but nice verbal discriminations, or the elucidations of curious and difficult passages. Of course the teacher should prepare himself to unfold, so far as he may, what is difficult or obscure in Scripture. But let him never forget that the main staple of his teaching should be concerning points that require none of this fine hair-splitting. The great fundamental doctrines of salvation are plain and easy of comprehension, and the passages which teach them are free from all obscurity. Our Saviour did not take his disciples through a labyrinth of rabbinical lore, while initiating them in the doctrines of his kingdom. His teachings were addressed to plain, unlettered men, and were taken from the most obvious and easily intelligible facts of common life. In studying these teachings now, while we would not disparage the rabbis, let us chiefly strive to take instruction, as Mary did, sitting at the feet of Jesus himself, listening to his own most wonderful words.

Take for instance the parable of the Sower. If, in the sacred record, or elsewhere, there were means of finding the exact locality, the very field, which was before the Saviour's eye when he uttered the parable, and if we could present to a class an exact geographical delineation of that field, and the evidence by which its identity was established, such information certainly would not be without its value. It would be curious and interesting. But the great beauty of the parable consists in the fact that the important truths which it contains and illustrates are quite independent of any particular locality. The teacher would certainly be unwise who should spend his ingenuity in trying to create a geographical, or antiquarian, or grammatical interest in the passage, rather than in applying its obvious and patent meaning to the common wants of men all around him.

I had occasion not long since to walk across an unenclosed common. The fences had been thrown down, and the tide of travel, instead of passing round the sides of the parallelogram, had made for itself a shorter route across lots. Here was a broad beaten path, trodden hard and smooth by the continual passage of men and beasts. Any child might understand that seed sown here, "by the wayside," would come to nothing. The thought occurred, if the heart of any one has become like this beaten path, so that the seed of God's word is lost upon it, what shall be done to bring about a change? How shall this indurated soil be made fit for receiving seed? What would a farmer do in such a case?

In the first place, he would *enclose* the spot. If the fences were once repaired, so that men and cattle could no longer trespass upon it, in a very few weeks, under the general laws of vegetation, the grass and herbs would spring up and cover the space which is now hard and bare. God has his enclosures around the heart for this very purpose. One of these is the holy Sabbath. God has hedged in this day by a divine command, to preserve it from all profane trespassing of worldly affairs.

If we would observe strictly his prohibitions, and let no worldly business or amusements enter this sacred enclosure, we would be driven almost necessarily to attend to religious subjects. The seed sown from the pulpit, or in the Sabbath-school, would have some chance of germinating, instead of being trodden under foot. But unfortunately we break down the hedge God has placed around the holy day, and let all sorts of objects intrude and trample upon the soil. Men allow their business to enter, boys their sports. The boy who goes a gunning, or fishing, or skating, or swimming on God's holy day, cannot be other than a wayside hearer. If the soil is ever to be in a condition to receive the sacred seed aright, in such a way as to give any hope of bearing fruit, first of all it must be *fenced in*. The time, which God has appointed for attending to religious truth, must be sacredly guarded from intrusion.

When a farmer has determined to reclaim a common, his first step, as already described, is to enclose it. The next thing to be done is *to break it up*. The hard, beaten tracks especially must be broken up. God has his methods of disturbing and breaking up the hardened soil of a worldly heart. Sickness, loss of property, death of friends, afflictions of various kinds, are among the means which God sometimes uses to render this stubborn, indurated surface yielding and penetrable to the truth. A man who finds himself in the condition of a confirmed "wayside" hearer, and who sincerely wishes to bring about a change, may sometimes produce a salutary effect upon himself by afflicting his own soul. Something is needed to disturb such a man, to break up the soil of his heart, and prepare it for the reception of the seed.

The next thing that the farmer would need, in reclaiming his common, would be the genial influence of the rain and the dew from heaven. The analogy in spiritual husbandry is obvious. The dews of divine grace must descend upon the soil, or all other means are in vain.

But it is not necessary to carry on the train of thought thus casually suggested. What it was meant to illustrate was this: Any teacher, of good sense and observation, with simply his New Testament before him, might interest and instruct a class of children, and teach them most important practical truths, without any great amount of learning. I would not discard Commentaries and Question Books. But I do beg of teachers to study more the direct words of Jesus. What you need, in preparing for your class, is not so much curious research, as *thought*. Do not study less, but meditate more. Let your own minds work upon the materials drawn directly from the Scriptures themselves. Remember the Sabbath-school is distinctively the BIBLE-school, the word of God being our great and main text-book; and whatever other books are used, they are best fitted to their purpose when they lead most to the diligent study of the holy Scriptures; and I cordially commend, to such as have the gifts to succeed in it, the example of those teachers who, while before their classes, teach directly from the sacred text, without reference to notes, commentaries, or question books.

XXXIV.

TEACHING CHILDREN WHAT THEY DO NOT UNDERSTAND.

It is not uncommon to hear persons declaim against teaching children what they do not understand. If by this is meant that children should not learn a set of words as parrots do, merely by the ear, and without attaching any idea to what they utter, no one will dissent from the propriety of the rule. But if the meaning is that they should learn nothing except what they fully comprehend, the rule certainly needs to be hedged in by some grave precautions.

There are indeed few things which any one, the oldest or the wisest, fully comprehends. Who knows what matter is? Certainly not the most eminent of philosophers. They do not pretend to know. We pick up a pebble. Who can tell what it is, absolutely? We say that it is something which has certain qualities. But even these we know mainly by negations. The pebble is hard, that is, it does *not* yield to pressure. It is opaque, that is, it does *not* transmit light. It is heavy, that is, it does *not* remain still, but goes towards the centre of the earth, unless intercepted by some interposing body.

Who knows the meaning, absolutely, of a single article of the creed? Certainly not the most eminent of divines. We know certain things about the great mysteries of the Godhead, and even these things we know not directly, but by certain faint, distant analogies, and we express our knowledge in terms chosen mainly from Scripture and arranged with care by wise and learned men. These venerable formularies, containing the most exact verbal expression which the church has been able to frame, of what the Scriptures teach about God and his ways, we commit to memory, and we repeat them with comfort and edification. But we do not pretend to penetrate the very essence of their meaning. Who by searching can find out God? One must be God himself to understand him.

We read that Christ was tempted of the devil in the wilderness. There are many things in this transaction which we may be said, in a certain sense, to know. But a man will not proceed far in analyzing this knowledge before he will discover that there are mysteries underlying the whole, which he cannot penetrate. He knows some of the surface relations of things. But the things themselves, in their essence, are unknown. Was Christ tempted, as the devil tempts us, by suggesting thoughts in the mind? Was the devil present in a bodily shape? Did he utter an audible voice, by undulating the air, as we do? Has he direct relations to matter, as we have? How could his offer of worldly power and riches be any real temptation to the Saviour, when Jesus knew that Satan had no power to make his offer good?

There are indeed few things, in revelation or out of revelation, in mind or in matter, which we really and fully comprehend. If, therefore, we are to teach children nothing but what they understand, we must either teach them nothing at all, or our rule must be materially qualified. No one knows absolutely but God. Among created beings, there are almost infinite gradations of intelligence, although the highest created intelligence begins its range infinitely below that of the Divine mind. A given formula of words, therefore, may express very different degrees of truth according to the degree of intelligence of the party using it. A catechism or a creed may convey twenty different degrees of meaning to twenty successive persons, varying in age, character, and culture. Yet the very youngest and feeblest shall understand something of its meaning, while the wisest and oldest shall not have exhausted it. The young and feeble intellect, receiving a formula of truth with suitable explanations of its terms, takes in at once a portion of its meaning, and gradually grows into a fuller comprehension of what it has received. A statement of doctrine received by a child at the age of five, conveys to him a few feeble rays of light. The same statement at the age of ten, means to him far more than it did before, while at twenty it is all luminous with knowledge.

The mind itself grows and expands, and with every addition to its own vigour and stature, does it find new truths in those expressive and pregnant formulas of doctrine with which it has from childhood been familiar. It is like looking at a material object, first with the naked eye, and then with glasses of continually increased magnifying power. The more we increase the power, the more we see in the same bit of matter. Yet no glass will ever reveal to us the very interior essence of even the smallest particle of dust. God only knows fully either any single thing, or the sum of things. Because, however, we cannot see into the essence of a pebble or a grain of sand, shall we shut our eyes to it altogether? Shall we not look at it, first as an infant does, then, as a child, then as a youth, then as a man, then as a philosopher? We can never see it as God does. But we shall see it with ever-growing powers of vision, until that which was to us at first only a rude mass become an exhaustless organized microcosm of wonders.

I do not advocate the overloading of children with verbal statements of abstruse doctrines, whether of religion or of science. Much less would I turn them into parrots, to repeat phrases to which they attach no meaning at all. But when it is demanded, on the other hand, that they shall learn nothing but what they understand, I demur. I ask for explanation of the rule. I insist that every statement of truth which they learn, even the most elementary, contains depths which neither they nor their teachers can fathom. I insist that both in science and religion, there are certain great, admitted elementary truths, reduced to forms of sound words with which the whole world is familiar; and that while these formularies contain many things which a child cannot understand, they yet contain many things of which even the youngest child has a fair comprehension. I insist that a carefully prepared religious creed or catechism, even though it contains many things beyond a child's present comprehension, is a fit subject for study. Memory in childhood is quick and tenacious. The treasures first laid away in that storehouse are the last to be removed. They may be overlaid by subsequent accumulations, but they are still there ready for use. Forms of sound words are certainly among the things which parents and teachers should store away in the young minds of which they have charge. If the child does not understand all that he thus places in his memory, he understands portions of it just as he sees certain qualities of the pebble which he holds in his hand, and he will see and understand more, as his mind expands and his powers of spiritual vision increase.

18

XXXV.

FAITH AS AN EDUCATIONAL POWER.

A THEORY of teaching much in vogue is that the young should receive nothing on trust. The theory may not be stated perhaps in this broad and unqualified manner. But if the methods and processes of the class-room be analyzed, it will be found that an idea of this kind lies at the bottom of what the teacher is attempting. The assumption seems to be, first, that a child should learn nothing but what he can comprehend, and secondly, that he should learn nothing but what he can prove. He is accordingly set to work to reason out everything that he studies. He is not required to learn plain and admitted truths and facts, on competent authority, but he must discover and invent everything for himself, as if the whole world of knowledge was a mere *terra incognita,* and he were the first explorer. He must torture his brain in finding reasons for every thing. He is not allowed to learn the multiplication table unless he can first demonstrate it. He is not allowed to say that 9 times 7 are 63, unless he can first contemplate the proposition concretely, as represented by piles of apples, or nuts, or other visible objects, and then abstractly as referring to pure entities and relations, and finally, unless he can explain the process of his own mind in reaching the result. There is undoubtedly a subtile tissue of metaphysics underlying the plain warp and woof of the multiplication table. A strictly logical expression of its meaning requires some nicety of diction and a considerable power of abstraction. But to restrain a child from learning the mere figures of the table and their practical uses in actual multiplication, until he can work out for himself, and can give to others, a complete expression of its relations, is like not letting a child learn to walk until he has discovered and can explain the mechanics of walking.

The theory is founded on the assumption that the cultivation of the reasoning faculty should precede the cultivation of the memory. It insists that nothing should be presented to the mind of a child to be accepted by him and committed to memory, until the child has first proved the thing to be true, or at least until a demonstration of its truth has been made to him. As a scheme of education, it ignores almost every cardinal fact in the history of the development of the human faculties.

In the first place, reasoning in regard to any intellectual process is much more readily and clearly apprehended by young persons, after they have become familiar with the process itself, as a practical rule. If the rule is first given by the teacher, as a mere working rule, and the child goes through it day by day, until every step of the process is perfectly familiar to the mind, the business of explaining the foundation of the rule is then comparatively easy. Often indeed the whole reason of it becomes self-evident, without explanation. A boy studying algebra, for instance, may be taught the formula of solving a quadratic equation, without any demonstration of the proposition which underlies the formula. It is not necessary that he should understand this demonstration, in order that he may solve equations by the formula. Indeed, the very best way for a young person to approach such a demonstration, is to begin with practical solutions under the rule. When the various steps of the process, and the terms employed, have thus become perfectly familiar, the mind seizes readily and clearly the reasoning on which the process is founded. Expertness in solving problems or in doing sums, is the surest and quickest way of reaching the underlying truths on which the solutions depend. Practice, in other words, should precede theory. This, I believe to be a sound principle of education; and every method of teaching which proceeds in the opposite direction, is working against nature.

In the second place, there is no fact more patent, even to the most casual observation, than that the memory is one of the very first faculties of the human mind to be developed. Children can commit to memory when they can do almost nothing else. Committing to memory, instead of being the painful drudgery that it becomes in later years, is in childhood a delight. The Creator seems to have arranged the order of the development of the faculties for this very purpose, that in our childhood and youth we may be chiefly occupied with the accumulation of materials in our intellectual storehouse. Now to reverse this process, to occupy the immature mind of childhood chiefly with reasoning, which is a faculty of later growth, and actually to put shackles and restraints upon the memory, is to ignore one of the primary facts of human nature. It is to be wiser than God.

In the third place, a child instinctively receives as true whatever his parent or teacher tells him. This instinctive faith of childhood is another of the primary facts of human nature, which the theory in question overlooks. The child, until taught otherwise, wants no higher reason for accepting any statement as true, than the fact that his father or mother or teacher has said so, and it is not merely unwise, but downright cruel, ruthlessly to crush out this faith of childhood. It is cruel to force the confiding young heart into premature skepticism by compelling him to hunt for reasons for everything, when he has reasons, to him all-sufficient, in the fact that his parents or teachers have told him so, or that he has so read it in the book which they have placed in his hands for his instruction. The child learns that he has a Father in heaven, not by a process of

18 *

reasoning, but by hearing it from his mother's lips. One leading object of the parental relation seems to be this very thing. The parent is, in the early years of childhood, to supply the mind, as well as the body, with food. The child receives either kind of food with equal and unquestioning faith. It is a part of the constitution of his nature to do so. It is the necessary counterpart to the other fact just named, that in those early years the memory is so active. In that spring-time of life, we receive without question whatever is told us, and we remember without effort whatever we receive; and our heavenly Father guards these first acquisitions from imposture by placing them under the direction of parental love. In other words, faith is one of the elementary powers in education, and any system of teaching is radically unwise which ignores or impairs it.

XXXVI.

THE PROPER USE OF AUTHORITY IN TEACHING.

It is not uncommon to hear ungodly and infidel people say that children should be left to grow up without any religious bias. When they have reached mature years, they can judge for themselves, and will then be free to choose their system of religion. To act otherwise, it is said, is making religion hereditary. Children are led to adopt blindly the religious opinions of their parents and teachers, on mere authority, from filial reverence, or passive indifference, without ever attaining to hearty and intelligent assent. Stephen Girard made this idea the basis of that stupendous practical cruelty which he attempted to connect with the administration of his princely munificence. This idea is connected with another, or rather it is part of another and more general idea, namely, that children should be taught no doctrine which they cannot fully understand. According to this theory, you must explain the rationale of every fact or truth before you require the child to commit it to memory. An extremist of this school would not even let a child learn the multiplication table, until it had mastered the subtle metaphysics of the science of numbers, and could explain exactly why seven times nine make sixty-three.

The whole theory rests upon a false idea of the processes of the human mind in learning. The Creator after all is the wisest teacher, and we do well to follow his instructions. God has made the child with the instinctive tendency to receive truth in the first place on mere authority. There is no attribute of childhood more obvious than this. The child believes implicitly what his father and mother tell him. Were it not for this principle of instinctive and implicit faith, it would be impossible to make those gigantic strides in knowledge which ordinarily mark every human being during the first years of its infantile and childish existence. This principle of faith seems implanted, and the parental relation established, for this very thing as one of its main ends. If the infant, the child, the youth, must accept nothing as truth but what it has first demonstrated to be true, and comprehended the exact rationale of it, the advancement in knowledge during our early years will be slow indeed.

How do we learn language in childhood? Is it not solely on authority, and by example? A child who lives in a family where no language is used but that which is logically and grammatically correct, will learn to speak with logical and grammatical correctness, long before it is able to give any account of the processes of its own mind in the matter, or indeed to understand those processes when explained by others. The parent who should take measures to prevent a child from speaking its mother tongue, except just so far and so fast as it could understand and explain the subtle logic which underlies all language, would be quite as wise as the one who should withhold from his child all religious doctrine, except so far as it can thoroughly understand it, and demonstrate its truth.

Even when a child is so far advanced as to begin the study of any subject as a science, the teacher who is wise will still teach him many mere arbitrary rules. Take arithmetic for example, and begin at the beginning. To have a really correct apprehension of the principle of the decimal notation, to understand how it is that we might in the same way take any other number than ten as the base of a numerical scale,—that we might increase, for instance, by fives, or eights, or nines, or twelves, just as well as by tens,—all this requires considerable maturity of intellect, and some subtlety of reasoning. Indeed we doubt whether one in ten of grown people, and of those who think they know arithmetic perfectly, have yet ever made an ultimate analysis of the first step in arithmetical notation. Very many of them, we doubt not, would open their eyes were we to tell them, for instance, that the number of fingers on a man's two hands may be just as correctly expressed by the figures 11, 12, 13, or 14, as by the figures 10. Yet so it is, as one may readily understand who is familiar with the generalizations of higher arithmetic and algebra. But it would be up-hill work to attempt to make the matter quite clear to a beginner. We wisely, therefore, give our children at first an arbitrary rule for notation. We give them an equally arbitrary rule for addition. They accept these rules and work upon them, and learn thereby the practical operations of arithmetic. The theory will follow in due time. When perfectly familiar with the practice and the forms of arithmetic, and sufficiently mature in intellect, they awake gradually and surely to the beautiful logic which underlies the science.

People, in reasoning on this subject, confound the process of education and growth with that of scientific research. The man with mind already mature, engaged in prosecuting original investigations, for the purpose of discovering new truths, proceeds by doubts and by analysis. Not so the child. He receives every thing at first on faith, and receives it just as it is presented, in concrete forms. A child learns an article of the creed or an answer in the catechism. That article or answer contains perhaps some theological doctrine expressed in most exact and fitting words. All that is contained in this significant formula he will not comprehend, any more than he comprehends the full mystery by which the figures 10 express correctly the number of fingers on his two hands. But he accepts the formula as true because his father or mother or teacher has told him it is true. God has given him in childhood the faculty and the necessity to receive what is so presented. Moreover, to a certain extent, this formula is intelligible to him. All forms of truth have in themselves a certain amount of self-evidencing power even to the youngest mind. The veriest child can understand something even of the mysterious doctrine of the Trinity. As we grow older and our minds become more mature, we gradually understand more and more of the infinite fulness of meaning embraced in these forms of sound words which we have learned in childhood.

There is no servility in thus teaching our children the truths which we ourselves believe and know. We do it in all every-day matters. We should do it in religious matters. God has made us parents for this very purpose.

THE END.

www.ingramcontent.com/pod-product-compliance
Lightning Source LLC
Chambersburg PA
CBHW020828230426
43666CB00007B/1146